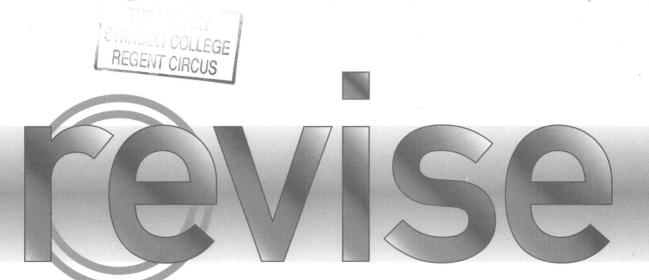

revise

GCSE
Spanish

Ana Kolkowska

with Tony Buzan

D1331981

Hodder & Stoughton

A MEMBER OF THE HODDER HEADLINE GROUP

Acknowledgments

The author and publishers would like to thank the following examination boards for permission to reproduce the following specimen exam material.

Northern Examinations and Assessment Board
GCSE Spanish Specimen Material 1998 Examination:
Listening Foundation Section A Questions 1–3, 5, 7–15 in Chapter 11 Listening exercises 1–13, Question 6 in Chapter 5 Foundation Task 1, Higher Questions 4–14 in Chapter 11 Listening exercises 14–24; *Speaking* Foundation and Higher Role Play 2 in Chapter 8 Higher Task 2; *Reading* Foundation Questions 1–5 in Chapter 11 Reading exercises 1–5, Question 6 in Chapter 10 Foundation Task 3, Question 9 in Chapter 11 Reading exercise 6, Higher Question 1 in Chapter 7 Higher Task 3, Questions 2, 4, 5, 8, and 10 in Chapter 11 Reading exercises 8–12; *Writing* Higher Question 2 in Chapter 11 Writing exercise 4.

EDEXCEL *London Examinations – Modern Foreign Languages Spanish Specimen Papers & Mark Schemes* G7/6: Paper 1F Listening and Responding Questions 12–16 in Chapter 1 Foundation Task 2 and Questions 30–34 in Chapter 10 Foundation Task 1, Paper 1H Listening and Responding Questions 26–31 in Chapter 10 Higher Task 1; Paper 2F and 2H Speaking Role Play A (1) in Chapter 11 Speaking exercise 1, Role Play C3 in Chapter 11 Speaking exercise 4; Paper 3F Reading and Responding Question 6 in Chapter 10 Foundation Task 3; Paper 4H Writing Question 2 in Chapter 9 Higher Task 3. Edexcel Foundation, London Examinations accepts no responsibility whatsoever for the accuracy or method of working in the answers given.

Reproduced by kind permission of the Midland Examining Group *Specimen Question Papers and Mark Schemes* **(June 1998 onwards) printed June 1995 © MEG (not including third party copyright material):** *Listening* Section 1 Exercise 3 Questions 7–11 in Chapter 8 Foundation Task 1, Section 2 Exercise 1 Questions 1–5 in Chapter 9 Higher Task 1, Exercise 2 Question 6 in Chapter 3 Foundation Task 1, Exercise 3 Question 11 in Chapter 7 Foundation Task 1. *Speaking* Role Play 1, Card 1 in Chapter 7 Foundation Task 2, Card 2 in Chapter 8 Foundation Task 2, Card 3 in Chapter 11 Speaking exercise 2, Card 4 in Chapter 6 Foundation Task 2, Role Play 2, Card 1 in Chapter 11 Speaking exercise 3, Card 4 in chapter 7 Higher Task 2. *Reading* Section 1, Exercise 1, Questions 3–4 in Chapter 7 Foundation Task 3, Section 2, Exercise 1, Questions 1–8 in Chapter 4 Higher Task 2. *Writing* Foundation Section 1 Questions 1–2 in Chapter 11 Writing exercises 1–2, Section 2 Question 1 in Chapter 9 Foundation Task 2, Higher Section 2 Question 2 in Chapter 10 Task 4. The Midland Examining Group bears no responsibility for the example answers to questions taken from its past and specimen question papers which are contained in this publication.

Southern Examining Group *1998 Examinations Spanish Modular Specimen Papers and Marking Schemes (issued January 1996):* Module 1 *Reading* Task 5 in Chapter 9 Higher Task 2, *Listening* Task 5 in Chapter 9 Foundation Task 1; Module 2 *Listening* Higher Question 2 in Chapter 8 Higher Task 1; Module 3 *Writing* Higher Task 3 in Chapter 7 Higher Task 4; Module 4 *Listening* Higher Question 1 in Chapter 2 Higher Task 2, Higher Question 3 in Chapter 3 Higher Task 1, *Speaking* Higher Tier only (page 142) in Chapter 10 Higher Task 2.

ISBN 0 340 66389 8

First published 1997

Impression number	10 9 8 7 6 5 4 3 2 1
Year	2001 2000 1999 1998 1997

The 'Teach Yourself' name and logo are registered trade marks of Hodder & Stoughton Ltd.

Designed and produced by Gecko Ltd, Bicester, Oxon Printed in Great Britain for Hodder & Stoughton Educational, a division of Hodder Headline Plc, 338 Euston Road, London NW1 3BH by Scotprint Ltd, Musselburgh, Scotland.

Mind Maps: Donna Kim-Brand
Illustrations: Karen Donnelly, Andrea Norton, John Plumb
Cover design: Amanda Hawkes
Cover illustration: Paul Bateman

Contents

Revision made easy

The four pages that follow contain a gold mine of information on how you can achieve success both at school and in your exams. Read them and apply the information, and you will be able to spend less, but more efficient, time studying, with better results. If you already have another *Hodder & Stoughton Revision Guide*, skim-read these pages to remind yourself about the exciting new techniques the books use, then move ahead to page 9.

This section gives you vital information on how to remember more *while* you are learning and how to remember more *after* you have finished studying. It explains

> **how to use special techniques to improve your memory**

> **how to use a revolutionary note-taking technique called Mind Maps that will double your memory and help you to write essays, use the language and answer exam questions**

> **how to read everything faster while at the same time improving your comprehension and concentration**

All this information is packed into the next four pages, so make sure you read them!

Your *amazing* memory

There are five important things you must know about your brain and memory to revolutionise your school life.

> **1** how your memory ('recall') works *while* you are learning

> **2** how your memory works *after* you have finished learning

> **3** how to use Mind Maps – a special technique for helping you with all aspects of your studies

> **4** how to increase your reading speed

> **5** how to zap your revision

1 Recall *during* learning – the need for breaks

When you are studying, your memory can concentrate, understand and remember well for between 20 and 45 minutes at a time. Then it *needs* a break. If you carry on for longer than this without one, your memory starts to break down! If you study for hours non-stop, you will remember only a fraction of what you have been trying to learn, and you will have wasted valuable revision time.

So, ideally, *study for less than an hour*, then take a five- to ten-minute break. During the break listen to music, go for a walk, do some exercise, or just daydream. (Daydreaming is a necessary brain-power booster – geniuses do it regularly.) During the break your brain will be sorting out what it has been learning, and you will go back to your books with the new information safely stored and organised in your memory banks. We recommend breaks at regular intervals as you work through the *Revision Guides*. Make sure you take them!

2 Recall *after* learning – the waves of your memory

What do you think begins to happen to your memory straight *after* you have finished learning something? Does it immediately start forgetting? No! Your brain actually *increases* its power and carries on remembering. For a short time after your study session, your brain integrates the information, making a more complete picture of everything it has just learnt. Only then does the rapid decline in memory begin, and as much as 80 per cent of what you have learnt can be forgotten in a day.

However, if you catch the top of the wave of your memory, and briefly review (look back over) what you have been revising at the correct time, the memory is stamped in far more strongly, and stays at the crest of the wave for a much longer time. To maximise your brain's power to remember, take a few minutes and use a Mind Map to review what you have learnt at the end of a day. Then review it at the end of a week, again at the end of a month, and finally a week before the exams. That way you'll ride your memory wave all the way to your exam – and beyond!

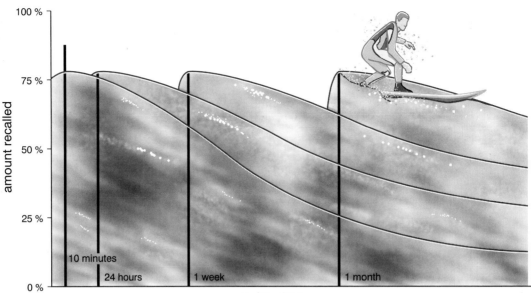

review time (x-axis)

amount recalled (y-axis): 100 %, 75 %, 50 %, 25 %, 0 %

10 minutes — 24 hours — 1 week — 1 month

Amazing as your memory is (think of everything you actually do have stored in your brain at this moment) the principles on which it operates are very simple: your brain will remember if it (a) has an image (a picture or a symbol); (b) has that image fixed and (c) can link that image to something else.

3 The Mind Map® – a picture of the way you think

Do you _like_ taking notes and making vocabulary lists? More importantly, do you like having to go back over and learn them before exams? Most students I know certainly do not! And how do you take your notes and make your lists? Most people take notes and make lists on lined paper, using blue or black ink. The result, visually, is _boring_! And what does your brain do when it is bored? It turns off, tunes out, and goes to sleep! Add a dash of colour, rhythm, imagination, and the whole note-taking process becomes much more fun, uses more of your brain's abilities, _and_ improves your recall and understanding.

A Mind Map mirrors the way your brain works. It can be used for note-taking and gathering vocabulary phrases and language structures from books or in class, for reviewing what you have just studied, for revising, and for essay planning for coursework and in exams.

It uses all your memory's natural techniques to build up your rapidly growing 'memory muscle'.

You will find Mind Maps throughout this book. Study them, add some colour, personalise them, and then have a go at drawing your own – you'll remember them far better! Put them on your walls and in your files for a quick-and-easy review of the topic.

How to draw a Mind Map

1. Start in the middle of the page with the page turned sideways. This gives your brain the maximum room for its thoughts.

2. Always start by drawing a small picture or symbol. Why? Because a picture is worth a thousand words to your brain. And try to use at least three colours, as colour helps your memory even more.

3. Let your thoughts flow, and write or draw your ideas on coloured branching lines connected to your central image. These key symbols and words are the headings for your topic. The Mind Map at the top of the next page shows you how to start.

4. Then add facts, further items and ideas, time markers and tenses by drawing more, smaller, branches on to the appropriate main branches, just like a tree.

5. Always print your word clearly on its line. Use only one word per line. The Mind Map at the foot of the next page shows you how to do this.

6. To link ideas and thoughts on different branches, use arrows, colours, underlining, and boxes.

How to read a Mind Map

1. Begin in the centre, the focus of your topic.

2. The words/images attached to the centre are like chapter headings: read them next.

3. Always read out from the centre, in every direction (even on the left-hand side, where you will have to read from right to left, instead of the usual left to right).

Using Mind Maps

Mind Maps are a versatile tool – use them for taking notes in class or from books, for solving problems, for brainstorming with friends, and for reviewing and revising for exams – their uses are endless! You will find them invaluable for planning essays for coursework and exams. Number your main branches in the order in which you want to use them and off you go – the main headings for your essay are done and all your ideas are logically organised!

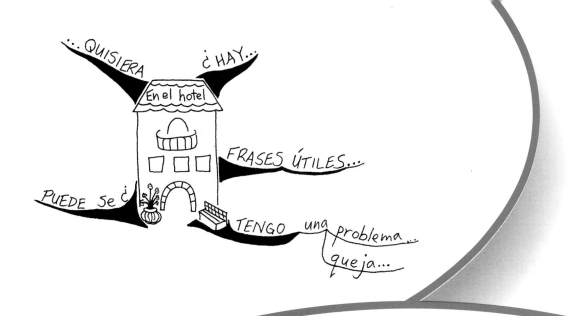

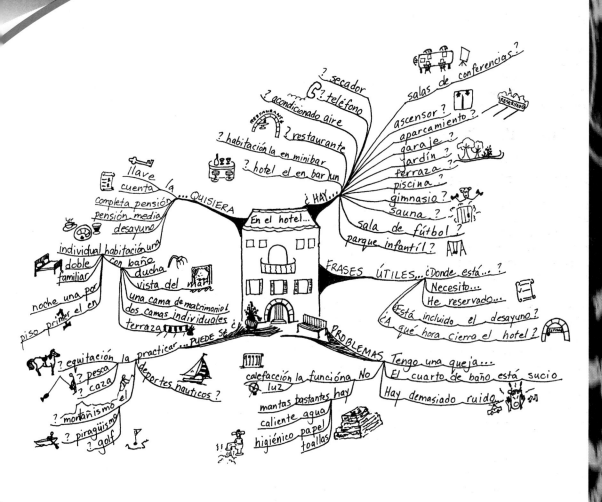

4 Super speed reading

It seems incredible, but it's been proved – the faster you read, the more you understand and remember! So here are some tips to help you to practise reading faster – you'll cover the ground more quickly, remember more, *and* have more time for revision!

★ Read the whole text (whether it's a lengthy book, a long passage or an exam paper) very quickly first, to give your brain an overall idea of what's ahead and get it working. (It's like sending out a scout to look at the territory you have to cover – it's much easier when you know what to expect!) Then read the text again for more detailed information.

★ Have the text a reasonable distance away from your eyes. In this way your eye/brain system will be able to see more at a glance, and will naturally begin to read faster.

★ Take in groups of words at a time. Rather than reading 'slowly and carefully' read faster, more enthusiastically. Your comprehension will rocket!

★ Take in phrases rather than single words while you read.

★ Use a guide. Your eyes are designed to follow movement, so a thin pencil underneath the lines you are reading, moved smoothly along, will 'pull' your eyes to faster speeds.

5 Helpful hints for exam revision

Start to revise at the beginning of the course. Cram at the start, not the end and avoid 'exam panic'!

Use Mind Maps throughout your course, and build a Master Mind Map for each subject – a giant Mind Map that summarises everything you know about the subject.

Use memory techniques such as mnemonics (verses or systems for remembering things like dates and events, or lists).

Get together with one or two friends to revise, compare Mind Maps, and discuss topics.

And finally...

★ *Have fun while you learn* – studies show that those people who enjoy what they are doing understand and remember it more, and generally do it better.

★ *Use your teachers* as resource centres. Ask them for help with specific topics and with more general advice on how you can improve your all-round performance.

★ *Personalise your* **Revision Guide** by underlining and highlighting, by adding notes and pictures. Allow your brain to have a conversation with it!

Your brain is an amazing piece of equipment – learn to use it, and you, like thousands of students before you will be able to master Spanish with ease. The more you understand and use your brain, the more it will repay you!

Tricks of the trade to make the grade!

How will this book help me?

This Spanish Revision Guide covers ten topics, and includes vocabulary and structures that you need to achieve good grades at GCSE for any of the exam boards. It presents the language in a way that is easy to grasp and to remember.

Find out from the start which tiers you have been entered for so that you can see which sections of the revision guide will be most useful to you. For example, you might be entered for Higher Listening, Speaking and Reading and Foundation Writing.

Use the checklist and Notes/Options

Work through each chapter: shade in or tick the Checklist (Fine or Help!). Then read through the Notes/Options paying particular attention to the items where you have shaded or ticked Help! and where you need to build your confidence. Once you have worked through the Notes/Options, have a go at the Test Yourself exercises at the end of each chapter tier. There are exercises within all four skills areas: Listening, Speaking, Reading, Writing.

Mark your answers using the key in the shaded boxes. If you haven't got a very good mark, check back to the chapter again. .

Make the most of the Mind Maps

Each of the ten topics is linked to the Mind Maps in the coloured section; these connect the ideas and vocabulary in the chapters to help you learn the vital vocabulary. Watch out for the signpost showing you the way to interesting Mind Maps. There is a summary Mind Map on page 97.

Have a go at making your own Mind Maps. Use symbols and pictures on them, it will really help you to retain the vocabulary and ideas. There are also grammar Mind Maps to help you to revise the crucial tenses.

A practice mock exam

Finally there is a mock exam in Chapter 11 that is a compilation of specimen exam questions taken from various exam boards. Follow the instructions given at the beginning of each section of the mock exam and try to complete the chapter in conditions as near as possible to a real exam. It is not a good idea, however, to do the whole mock exam in one sitting. Make sure you have breaks in between each section.

When you have finished the Listening, Reading, Speaking and Writing sections mark your answers. Take special care over the Writing and Speaking mark schemes. They are complicated but knowing the standards demanded by the exam boards will help you achieve the grade you want.

A grammar reference

You will find the grammar explanations in Chapter 12 very useful as your revision progresses.

Train your memory

Plan out the time before your exam so that you revise a little every day allowing your mind to absorb the information. Give more time to the topics that you find most difficult. Bear in mind the other subjects you are taking; juggle your revision time carefully.

Some people find that they are most receptive to learning and memorising in the mornings, but only you can decide what works best for you. Be aware of what are the hardest topics and structures for you, and don't leave them to the last minute!

TOP TEN TIPS for learning vocabulary

1 Use different coloured pens to highlight masculine and feminine words on Mind Maps.
2 Draw an item or symbol for key vocabulary.
3 Don't try to learn more than ten words at a time.
4 Take ten minutes to make a Mind Map. Then, after a break, take another ten minutes to write out the vocabulary using the Mind Map.

5 Use a list of ten words, start at the bottom and work upwards, as well as downwards.

6 Visualise each item of vocabulary as you say the word in Spanish.

7 Record yourself – play it back and imagine the item again.

8 Ask friends and family to test you on vocabulary.

9 Remember that with regular effort you can build a bigger vocabulary and recall it.

10 Think positive. Vocabulary is the key and the more often you learn small chunks, the easier it gets.

Are you sitting comfortably?

You need to be at ease when you are revising. Here are some tips to help you choose an ideal working environment.

LOCATION Never revise in the kitchen or the living room with the TV on or with brothers or sisters around. Find a place that is quiet and where there are no distractions. If you find it hard to revise at home, you could go to your library.

LIGHTING Natural light is best. If you can, sit by a window, If you have to work in artificial light, try to use a lamp rather than fluorescent lighting as this can give you eye strain. Avoid shadows; make sure that the light comes from your left if you are right-handed, and from your right if you are left-handed.

HEATING If you are too warm while you are revising, you might find that you start falling asleep – not ideal for training your memory! Fresh air helps concentration so open the windows while you are working, or at least during your short breaks.

SPACE Organise your desk or table so that your books, notes, dictionaries, pens and paper are within easy reach. If you have to keep getting up to look for things you will be easily distracted.

POSITION Make sure your chair is at the right height and that it is keeping your back straight while you are revising. You might get back-ache if you sit awkwardly. Never work in an armchair or lying on your bed: you will be too relaxed to take much in!

FUEL Meals are very important. Pay as much attention to your food intake as does an athlete training for a competition! Limit the amount of sugary and fatty things you eat as these increase irritability and can disrupt concentration. Likewise, stimulating drinks (such as coffee and tea) can revive you in the short term, but they might also disturb your sleep pattern and affect your memory if you're tired.

During the exam

• Structure your time so that you have enough time to answer all of the questions. Don't spend too long on one question. First answer the questions you can do easily and then go back to the more difficult ones.

• Answer all the questions.

• Look carefully at the number of marks you can get for each question. For example three marks means you must give three items of information in your answer.

• Stick to the point. Give opinions and reasons wherever you can and use the different tenses where appropriate. Don't pad out your answer with irrelevant material, it will be obvious that you can't answer the question.

• Plan your answers, especially for the Writing paper. Draw a quick Mind Map.

• Write clearly. Ask for some blank sheets if you want to write out notes or plan using a Mind Map. Remember to cross out neatly any work you don't want the examiner to mark.

• Leave some time at the end to look over your answers and for a final dictionary check.

• Remember to answer in the correct language!

Rubrics and instructions

Here is a list of the types of rubrics and instructions you might come across in the exam papers. Familiarise yourself with them so that you don't waste time looking up words in the dictionary during the exam. Failing to understand instructions might mean lost marks.

¿A qué hora...?	= At what time...?
... abre?	= ... open(s) / does it open?
... cierra?	= ... close(s) / does it close?
Añade	= Add
Apunta	= Note / write down
Busca en el diccionario	= Find in the dictionary
Cada una de estas frases contiene un error	= Each of these sentences has a mistake
Cambia / Corrige	= Change / Correct
... los detalles	= ... the details
¿Cierto o falso?	= True or false?
¿Cómo es / son?	= What is it / are they like?

Compara	= Compare
Completa	= Complete
... la conversación	= ... the conversation
... el formulario	= ... the form
Contesta las preguntas	= Answer the questions
... en español / ingés / cifras	= ... in Spanish / English / numbers
Copia / Corrige	= Copy / Correct
... los detalles	= ... the details
¿Cuáles de	= Which of
... las explicaciones corresponden a ...?	= ... the explanations correspond to / match ...?
¿Cuál es tu actitud hacia ...?	= What is your attitude toward ...?
¿Cuáles son	= What are
... las diferecias entre ...?	= ... the differences between ...?
... las ventajas / los inconvenientes?	= ... the advantages / disadvantages?
¿Cuándo?	= When?
¿Cuánto/a / s?	= How much / many?
Cuenta	= Tell / recount
Da	= Give
... información, razones	= ... information, reasons
... las gracias	= 'thank you'...
tu opinión sobre ...	= ... your opinion on ...
Decide cómo	= Decide how to
Di	= Say
Dibuja / Diseña	= Draw / Design
¿Dónde / Adónde?	= Where?
¿Dónde se pueden leer / oír estas frases?	= Where can you read / hear these sentences?
Empareja	= Pair / Match up
Encuentra / Busca	= Find
Escribe	= Write
... algunas frases	= ... some sentences
... el número	= ... the number
... la letra (que corresponde)	= ... the (matching) letter
... una carta	= ... a letter
... una lista	= ... a list
... una postal	= ... a postcard
... una respuesta	= ... a reply / answer
Escoge / Elige	= Choose
... la descripción que corresponde mejor	= ... the description that is closest
Escucha la cinta	= Listen to the cassette
Estudia el cuadro	= Look carefully at the box
¿Estás de acuerdo / en contra?	= Do you agree / disagree?
Explica / Justifica	= Explain / Justify
... tu opinión	= ... your opinion
Habla	= Speak
Haz preguntas	= Ask questions
Haz el papel de ...	= Play the role of ...
Haz un anuncio	= Make an announcement
Haz un diálogo	= Act out a dialogue
Haz un resumen	= Summarise
Haz una comparación	= Make a comparison
Haz una lista	= Make a list
Haz una entrevista	= Conduct an interview
He aquí	= Here is
... la siguiente información	= ... the following information
Indica / Marca	= Mark
... con una equis / una marca	= ... with a cross / tick
... sí o no	= ... yes or no
Lee	= Read
... el anuncio	= the advertisement
Menciona	= Mention
Mira el póster	= Look at the poster
No necesitarás todas las palabras	= You will not need all the words
Opinar	= To have an opinion / To think
Ordena / Pon en orden	= Put in (the correct) order

La palabra subrayada no es correcta.	= The underlined word is incorrect.
Escribe la palabra correcta.	= Write the correct word.
Para	= For
... cada pregunta	= ... each question
... persona	= ... person
... cliente	= ... customer
Pasa la hoja pagina	= Turn the page
Pide / Pregunta	= Ask (for)
Pon una equis / marca	= Put a cross / tick
... en la casilla correcta	= ... in the correct box
... en todas las casillas correctas	= ... in all the correct boxes
Pon una señal así (✔)	= Tick
Pregúntale lo que ...	= Ask him / her what...
Prepara una presentación oral sobre ...	= Prepare a spoken presentation on ...
Preséntate	= Introduce yourself
¿Qué	= What
... conclusiones sacas de ...?	= ... conclusions can you draw from ...?
... diferencias hay entre ...?	= ... differences are there between ...?
... significa(n)?	= ... does it / do they mean?
¿Quién habla?	= Who is speaking?
Quieres escribir a ...	= You want to write to ...
Rellena	= Fill in
... la tabla	= ... the table
... los espacios / blancos	= ... the spaces
... el formulario / la ficha	= ... the form
Respuestas	= Answers
Saluda al examinador / la examinadora	= Greet the examiner
Según la información	= According to the information
Siguientes	= Following
Sólo una de estas frases es correcta.	= Only one of these sentences is correct.
Subraya	= Underline

Sugiere	= Suggest
Tienes que	= You have
... corregir	= ... to correct
... escribir	= ... to write
Verdad / Mentira / No se sabe	= True / False / Not known
Y ahora, ¡a ti!	= It's your turn now!

Using a dictionary in the exam

TIME Try not to use your dictionary too much in the exam, you will waste a lot of time. Don't look up every word you don't understand. Look up only the words you really need.

VERBS Remember that verbs only appear in the infinitive. For example, you will not find hiciste (you did), but you will find hacer (to do).

ADJECTIVES Remember that adjectives appear in the masculine singular form. For example, you will not find largas, but you will find largo.

ABBREVIATIONS Make sure you are familiar with abbreviations and symbols used in dictionaries. For example 'n' is noun, 'f' is feminine, 'adj' is adjective. Dashes also represent the root of the word in some cases: español would mean Spanish and 'los -es' would represent los españoles (the Spanish).

CROSS-REFERENCING You might be given a list of choices for one word. In order to pick the correct one cross check between the Spanish-English and English-Spanish.

- Remember that having a dictionary in the exam is no substitute for learning vocabulary. Language is constructed by phrases and structures and not by individual words. Writing a sentence by looking up every word in the dictionary only results in your writing unintelligible rubbish. No examiner fooled.

LAST MINUTE The best thing you can do with the dictionary is to leave some time at the end of the exam to look up words you are not sure of.

Avoiding the dictionary

CONTEXT Make sure you understand the question; it might ask you for details or for a general impression. When you are reading or listening to a section keep an eye, or an ear, out for the words which will actually answer the question – you can almost ignore the rest. If you don't understand a word, try to work out what it means from its context. The rest of the words in the sentence will give you clues.

STRUCTURE Use your knowledge of grammar structure; look for tenses, plurals and adjectives to help you work out what a sentence is about.

SPANISH LIFESTYLE Use your knowledge of Spanish life and customs. For example, you may know that the Spanish have dinner late in the evening. For a question asking you what time a Spaniard has dinner, knowing that the answer will most likely be a later time than is usual in Britain will help you listen out of an appropriate time.

TRAPS Look out for words which are similar in English and Spanish such as la policía (police) and el tráfico (traffic). Look out also for differences in Spanish and English spellings as in the following examples: foto (photo), estudiar (to study), teatro (theatre), catedral (cathedral). But beware of words that are similar in both languages but have different meanings, as with, for example, simpático which means friendly in English.

BRIDGES If you don't understand a word, look at its construction; what is at the beginning and at the end of the word? For example, you may not know the word carnicería, but if you recognise that carne means meat and that -ería on the end of a word indicates the shop where the item is sold, you can work out that carnicería means butcher's.

INITIATIVE If you can't remember a word, especially in the Writing and Speaking papers, don't invent one or use an English word. Try to get round it by using other Spanish words and phrases, for example, tienda grande instead of grandes almacenes and necesito folletos rather than le ruego me mande folletos.

The mock exam

BEFORE YOU START

1 Can you understand the Spanish instructions? If not, look at the Rubrics and Instructions in this section.
2 Have you got ready the following items: clock, Spanish-English dictionary, at least two good pens and plenty of paper for notes and ideas?
3 Listening Paper: have you got the cassette in the machine and is it positioned at the correct place on Side 2?
4 Speaking Test: have you got a blank cassette in another machine to enable you to record your answers and mark yourself? If this is not possible, ask a friend to mark you, or mark yourself after each question so that you don't forget what you have said.

During the mock exam

INSTRUCTIONS Follow the instructions at the beginning of each section carefully.
TIME Give yourself the stated time allotted for using the dictionary as instructed.

DICTIONARY Don't look up every word of a sentence you don't understand. Look up nouns and remember that you will only find a verb in the infinitive in the dictionary. Remember which verb endings correspond to particular tenses and persons.
SHOW OFF Make sure you show you can use past and future tenses as well as present tenses.
TAKE A BREAK Give yourself a break between each paper!

What's my grade?

If you want to know what grade you have achieved in the mock exam, follow this scheme.

How do I add up my totals? Each paper is worth 25% of the total score. Use a calculator to help you work out your scores for each paper. You must add up the marks for the questions you were required to do and turn the total into a percentage.

For the Speaking Test add together your totals for the role plays and then turn the total into a percentage.

Add up the totals of each of the four papers (Listening, Speaking, Reading, Writing) and divide it by four to get your final percentage.

How do I turn the totals into a percentage? If you have a pocket calculator enter your total marks for the section, divide it by the maximum marks for the section and multiply it by 100. The answer is your percentage for that test. For example: $18 \div 25 \times 100 = 72\%$. The percentages are then converted to a final grade.

Foundation		Higher	
Grade	*%*	**Grade**	*%*
G	1–20	**D**	1–25
F	21–40	**C**	26–50
E	41–60	**B**	51–75
D	61–80	**A**	76–100
C	81–100		

Are you happy with your result?

¡**Enhorabuena!** If you have achieved a result of more than 75% of the total score (Foundation or Higher) and you are happy with your result, you can relax. Just spend half an hour a day doing general reading in Spanish, until a day or two before your exam.

For final revision: look at the Notes/Options for each chapter. Look through Mind Maps you have made, and those on pages 97–128. Have a final quick read through Chapter 12.

Are you unhappy with your result?

Don't despair, follow these guidelines and you will improve your results

If you feel that a certain skill has let you down (Listening, Speaking, Reading or Writing), concentrate your revision on improving that skill. If you feel that you have not shown sufficient knowledge of a particular topic, concentrate your revision on that topic. Use the Mind Maps on pages 97–128 to help you revise and check your knowledge by creating your own Mind Maps. If a poor understanding and use of tenses has let you down, check Chapter 12 (Grammar) and learn the tenses.

If you think you could have got a better grade if you had been able to express opinions and expand on basic points, go back to the Checklists and concentrate your efforts on the Notes/Options that deal with opinions and develop discussion.

Last minute tips!

Listening
• Remember that you don't need to write in full sentences.
• Look carefully at the pictures in the questions.
• If you miss a question, don't panic, keep listening, you can have another go in the second listen through.
• Write in the correct language.
• Don't worry too much about spelling as long as your answer is clear.
• If you are required to answer questions in Spanish, you will not be marked for the accuracy of the language.

Speaking
• Practise your presentation and topics using a cassette recorder and with friends until you can speak confidently and without hesitation.
• Remember that in the exam, once you have spoken, there is not much opportunity to go back and correct what you have said. Nor is it possible to leave a difficult question that you might get till last. It is better to have clear in your mind what you are going to say. Pause for a few moments before you speak and order what you are going to say. Perhaps try to recall a Mind Map.

• Once you start to speak, do so confidently.
• If you don't understand a question or want something repeated, say so: No comprendo, or Puede repetir, por favor.
• Try to spot the unexpected in the role plays.
• Remember to give opinions and reasons at every opportunity.
• Try to sound as spontaneous as possible and keep talking. If you rely on the examiner to prompt you with questions you might get asked a question you don't understand!
• Let the conversation flow, don't just *answer* questions, *ask* questions as well!

Reading
• Don't use a dictionary to look up every word you don't know. Check back to the *Avoid the dictionary* section in this introduction.
• Answer in the correct language!
• Marks will not be taken off for incorrect spellings as long as your answer is clear.
• Don't miss out questions. You are more likely to get a mark if you make an intelligent guess rather than leave a gap.
• If you are required to answer questions in Spanish, you will not be marked for the accuracy of the language.
• Don't spend too much time on each question as you might run out of time for other questions. You can always go back to a question when you've gone through the rest of the paper.

Writing
• Read the questions at least twice before you begin.
• Check the instructions using a dictionary if necessary.
• Plan your answer using a Mind Map so that you cover all the points required by the question.
• Do not use the dictionary to try out new expressions. Your are more than likely to get them wrong. It is better to stick to what you know and can say well.
• Don't spend too much time on each question as you might run out of time for other questions. You can always go back to a question when you've gone through the rest of the paper.
• Remember to give opinions and reasons at every opportunity.

Are you ready? ¡Buena suerte!

Ana Kolkowska

1

Información personal

All about me!

Wherever you have selected Help! in the checklist, make the most of the Notes/Options and the Mind Maps to build your confidence. The signposts will tell you where to find a Mind Map to help you learn the vocabulary you need.

SABADO →
← EL VIAJE
↑ EL COLEGIO
FOUNDATION ↘
↗ TEMPO LIBRE
HIGHER ↑

Help is at hand!

Notes/Options

1 ¿Cómo te llamas?
Me llamo …

¿Cómo se escribe tu nombre?
Se escribe - M - I - G - U - E - L.   *Make sure you know how to pronounce the alphabet.*

nombre   = name
apellido   = surname

2 ¿De qué nacionalidad eres?
Soy inglés(a).   escocés(a)
                         irlandés(a)
                         galés(a)
                         Girls add an 'a'!

3 ¿Cuántos años tienes?

Tengo 16 años.   16 = dieciseis, not sesenta (60)

edad   = age

¿Cuándo es tu cumpleaños? = When is your birthday?

Es el quince de noviembre.

Do you remember all of these months?

enero	mayo	septiembre
febrero	junio	octubre
marzo	julio	noviembre
abril	agosto	diciembre

fecha de nacimiento   = date of birth

checklist
What you need to know

How confident do you feel about each of these questions? Can you:

	Fine	Help!
1 say and spell your name?		
2 give your nationality?		
3 give your age and birthday?		
4 describe yourself (physical appearance and character)?		
5 give the same details about your family?		
6 talk about your pets (size, number and colour)?		
7 say where you live and spell it out?		
8 say how you feel (ill, well, tired, hungry, thirsty, cold, hot, better)?		
9 say where you have a pain?		
10 ask for items at a chemist's?		
11 call for help?		

4 ¿Cómo eres? = What are you like?

bastante = quite

ni … ni … = neither … nor …

Soy alto(a). alto(a) = tall
bajo(a) = short

Soy delgado(a). delgado(a) = slim
gordo(a) = fat
fuerte = strong build

Soy moreno(a). moreno(a) = dark
(hair and skin)
rubio(a) = fair (hair and skin)
negro(a) = black
blanco(a) = white
mestizo(a) = mixed race
pelirojo(a) = redhead

Tengo los ojos castaños. = I have brown eyes.
azules = blue
verdes = green
negros = dark brown

When describing your eyes you add an 's' at the end of the colour.

Tengo el pelo castaño. = I have brown hair.
rubio = blond
negro = black

Tengo el pelo largo. largo = long
corto = short
liso = straight
rizado = curly
ondulado = wavy
rapado = shaved

When describing your hair you add an 'o' at the end of the colour or describing word.

Soy simpático(a). simpático(a) = friendly
tímido(a) = shy
animado(a) = lively

Tengo buen sentido del humor. el sentido del humor
= sense of humour

5 ¿Tienes hermanos? = Do you have brothers or sisters?

Tengo un hermano mayor
y dos hermanas menores. mayor(es) = older
menor(es) = younger

Soy hijo(a) único(a). = I'm an only child.
hermanastro(s) = stepbother(s)
hermanastra(s) = stepsister(s)

Mi hermano se llama Felipe.
Es simpático e inteligente.

'Y' becomes 'e' in front of a word beginning with 'i'.

Mis hermanas se llaman
Elena y María.

se llaman = they are called

Son guapas y artísticas.
guapo/a(s)

son = they are
= attractive

Felipe tiene 18 años.

Not 'Felipe es 18 años'.

Cristina y María tienen 10 y
12 años.

'N' on the end of a verb describes more than one person, i.e. tiene = he/she has, tienen = they have.

¿Cómo es tu madre / padre? padre = father
madre = mother
padres = parents

Mi madre se llama Teresa.
Es muy trabajadora y cariñosa.
trabajador/a(es/as) = hard working
cariñoso/a(s) = affectionate

Mi padre se llama Tomás.
Es muy tranquilo.
tranquilo/a(s) = calm, easy going

Revise numbers 1 – 100, make sure you know all the ages of your family!

1 un/uno/una	11 once	21 veintiuno
2 dos	12 doce	22 veintidós
3 tres	13 trece	30 treinta
4 cuatro	14 catorce	31 treinta y uno
5 cinco	15 quince	40 cuarenta
6 seis	16 dieciséis	41 cuarenta y uno
7 siete	17 diecisiete	50 cincuenta
8 ocho	18 dieciocho	60 sesenta
9 nueve	19 diecinueve	70 setenta
10 diez	20 veinte	80 ochenta
		90 noventa
		100 cien

Uno/a becomes un when it is used in front of a noun starting with a vowel. E.g. Tiene un año.

6 ¿Tienes un animal en casa?   = Do you have a pet?

No, no tengo animal en casa.
No tengo mascota.

Sí, tengo un perro.   un perro = dog
un gato = cat

Se llama Toto. Es blanco y
negro. Tiene dos años.

See the Mind Map on page 99 to
revise animals.

7 ¿Dónde vives?   = Where do you live?

Vivo en 49 Park Road.

¿Cómo se escribe?   = How do you spell it?

Se escribe P-A-R-K R-O-A-D.   domicillo = address

Listen to the Alphabet on the cassette (Side 1,
Chapter 1). Check that you can spell out your
name and address. Practise spelling the names of
people in your family.

8 ¿Qué tal? / ¿Cómo estás?   = How are you?

¿Cómo te sientes?   = How do you feel?

Estoy bien.

Estoy estupendamente,
muy bien, bien, regular, mal,
muy mal, fatal

Me siento mal / bien.   = I don't feel well. /
I feel well.

Estoy malo/a.   = I'm ill.

Estoy cansado/a.   = I'm tired.

Tengo hambre.   = I'm hungry.

Tengo sed.   = I'm thirsty.

Tengo calor.   = I'm hot.

Me siento mejor / peor.   = I feel better / worse.

Have a look at the Mind Map on page 100
to revise how you feel in more depth!

How's your memory?

Talking about age, eyes and hair

Tengo	16 años
Tiene	los ojos castaños
Tienen	el pelo corto y liso

Describing size and character

Soy	alto/a, bajo/a, delgado/a, fuerte
Es	simpático/a
Son	inteligentes

For girls replace o *with* a *as ending.*

Going for a C?

Add simple opinions to your descriptions
and give a simple reason why, such as:

odio
no me gusta nada
no me gusta
me gusta
me gusta mucho
me encanta

Learn describing words such as simpático
and egoista so that you can say why you
like or dislike something.

Revise the parts of the body. Look at
the Mind Map on page 101 to help you.

9 ¿Dónde te duele? / ¿Dónde le duele? = Where do you (tú) / (usted) have a pain?

Remember that the tú form is used for talking to family and people your own age and that the usted form is used for talking to older people who you don't know.

¿Qué te duele? / ¿Qué le duele? = What hurts?

Me duele la cabeza. / Tengo dolor de cabeza. = I have got a headache.

Me duelen las muelas. = *Add an 'n' ending to the verb, because in Spanish you refer to teeth (more than one).*

10 ¿Qué desea? / ¿En qué puedo ayudarle? = How can I help you?

¿Tiene tiritas? = Do you have any plasters?

aspirinas = aspirins
jarabe para la tos = cough syrup
pastillas = tablets

¿Quiere un paquete / una caja / una botella grande? = Do you want a big packet / box / bottle?

No, un paquete pequeño.

11 ¿Necesita ayuda? = Do you need help?

¡Socorro! = Help!

Test yourself

Task 1

Rellena la ficha con tus datos personales.
(Fill in this form with your personal details.)

NOMBRE:
APELLIDO:
EDAD:
FECHA DE NACIMIENTO:
DOMICILIO:
Nº DE TELEFONO:

Task 2   LA FAMILIA

Try this listening question (Side 1, Chapter 1).

Rellena los espacios en blanco con los nombres de los jóvenes que hablan. Ejemplo: Ana

1 _____
2 _____
3 _____
4 _____
5 _____

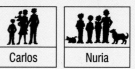

Ana   Jorge   Magdelena

Carlos   Nuria   Montse

Task 3

Escribe una carta a tu amigo/a español/a describiéndote a ti y a tu familia. (Write a short letter to a Spanish friend about you and your family, using 60-80 words.)

Look back at the Checklist.

When you have finished ask a friend who is also learning Spanish to read it. Can they understand it? Give yourself a point for every detail they understand (e.g. Tengo un hermano. = 1 point).

Do you remember these?

Letter writing to a friend:-

Start off: Querido + boy's name
              Querida + girl's name
Finish off: Un saludo / Abrazos

Información personal

All about me!

Make sure you can talk in detail about yourself, your family and friends and your lifestyle. If you don't feel confident about describing and giving opinions at this level, use the models to help you. This topic in particular lends itself to Mind Mapping (check the Maps on pages 98–101). Draw your own Mind Maps to describe yourself, your family, your friends and your attitudes towards a healthy lifestyle.

Help is at hand!

Notes/Options

1 *Check back to the Foundation Checklist. If you feel confident, carry on!*

2 Describe a tu mejor amigo/a.

Se llama Juan/Juana. Tiene quince años. No es ni alto/a ni bajo/a. Es moreno/a. Tiene el pelo marrón y corto. Tiene los ojos negros.

Es muy divertido/a. A veces me molesta pero generalmente me hace reír.

divertido = funny
a veces = sometimes

Me hace reír.

= He / She makes me laugh.

3 ¿Te llevas bien con tu/s padre/s / hermano/a/s / madre?

= Do you get on with your …?

Sí, me llevo bien con él / ella / ellos/as.

con él = with him
con ella = with her

No, no me llevo bien con él / ella / ellos/as.

No, no nos entendemos.

= No, we don't get on.

checklist
What you need to know

Can you:

 Fine Help!

1 answer the questions on the Foundation Checklist on page 15?

If you've ticked the Help! box, go back to the Foundation Notes/Options and revise!

2 describe your friends (physical appearance, character)?

3 say how you feel about your family and friends?

4 make arrangements to see a doctor or a dentist?

5 ask and answer questions about medical treatment?

6 give details about your lifestyle (healthy / unhealthy)

How is your memory?

Reasons for liking	
Me gusta porque	es simpático/a es divertido/a me ayuda me hace reír tiene buen sentido del humor me presta sus cosas = lends me his / her things

Reasons for disliking	
No me gusta porque	es antipático/a es aburrido/a es esgoista me molesta tiene mal humor me quita las cosas =takes away my things

4 Quisiera ver al médico / dentista / el farmacéutico. = I'd like to see the doctor / dentist / pharmacist.

Es urgente.

¿Puede darme hora para una visita esta tarde / mañana por la mañana? = Can I make an appointment for this afternoon / tomorrow morning?

5 Look at the medical instructions vocabulary on page 101 and learn these phrases:

¿Qué debo hacer? = What should I do?

¿Me puede recomendar algo? = Can you suggest anything?

¿Me debo quedar en la cama? = Should I stay in bed?

¿Necesito tomar algo / algún medicamento? = Should I take anything / any medicine?

¿Es necesario ver un médico? = Should I see a doctor?

¿Es necesario una receta médica? = Do I need a prescription?

6 ¿Tienes un régimen equilibrado? = Do you have a healthy diet?

¿Estás en forma? = Are you fit?

Sí, como bien. Como de todo: carne, pescado, fruta, legumbres, productos lácteos. de todo = a bit of everything
productos lácteos = dairy products

No me salto las comidas. = I don't skip meals.

No como demasiados dulces. = I don't eat too many sweet things.

Es malo / bueno para la salud. = It is bad / good for your health.

No debes / No se debe … = You shouldn't …

fumar / beber demasiado = to smoke / to drink too much

alcol / tomar drogas … = alcohol / to take drugs

porque es malo para la salud. = because it is bad for your health.

Me acuesto temprano. = I go to bed early.

Hago / practico deporte tres veces a la semana. = I do sports three times a week.

Going for an A?

Be prepared to talk about what you eat / don't eat and which sports you do (when and how often).

Be ready to give your opinion and say why.

Make the most of your memory!

Opinion 'starters'

Pienso que es peligroso para la salud.
es malo
es bueno

¿por qué? = why? por que = because

Cómo evitar el estrés …

trabaja un rato

come bien y haz un poco de ejercicio

estudia un rato y descansa un rato

duerme 7 horas

Test yourself

Task 1

Listen to the cassette (Side 1, Chapter 1, Higher) and answer the following questions in English.

1 Who does the woman want to see?

2 When can she have an appointment?

3 At what time is her appointment?

4 Why does she want an appointment?

Task 2

Lee la descripción de las ventajas del ejercicio y las precauciones que se deben tomar. Empareja los dibujos a seis de los puntos. (Read the following description of the advantages of and precautions for taking regular exercise. Match the 8 pictures to 8 of the items. E.g. A = 9.)

VENTAJAS E INCONVENIENTES DEL EJERCICIO FISICO
1 Produce sensación de bienestar.
2 Contribuye a mejorar la concentración, el apetito y el sueño.
3 Previene el estreñimiento.
4 Reduce o evita la obesidad.
5 Mejora el equilibrio y la coordinación.
6 Ayuda a que desaparezcan los dolores articulares y musculares.
7 Si padece alguna enfermedad, consulte antes al médico.
8 Si fuma, disminuya el consumo o abandone por completo el hábito.
9 No haga ejercicio después de una comida copiosa.
10 No realice movimientos bruscos y violentos.
11 No haga ejercicio si está muy cansado o se encuentra mal.

Look for key words that you should know such as: médico, sueño, dolores, comida, fumar, está cansado, se encuentra mal. Look for words that are similar in English such as: apetito, obesidad, concentración, violentos, abandone, hábito, coordinación.

Task 3

Imagine that you have been suffering from a sore throat since yesterday. You visit a pharmacy and ask the pharmacist for advice. She recommends some medication. You ask her how often you should take it and if you should see a doctor.

1 Saluda a la farmacéutica y explícale tus símptomas.

2 Dile desde cuándo te sientes mal.

3 Te recomienda un medicamento, pero no te explica como tomarlo. ¿Qué le preguntas?

4 Pregúntale si debes ver a otra persona.

Task 4

Escribe un artículo (unas 100 palabras) sobre el régimen ideal para mantener la salud. (Write an article about the ideal healthy diet using about 100 words.)

Learn the phrases in the Notes/Options 6 before you begin the task.

Answers

TASK 1
1 Doctor; 2 Tomorrow; 3 10 am; 4 Sunburn.

TASK 2
A 9; B 8; C 4; D 11; E 7; F 6; G 1.

TASK 3 (suggested answers)
1 Buenos días. Me siento mal. Me duele la garganta. ¿Me puede recomendar algo?
2 Me duele desde ayer.
3 ¿Cuántas veces al día debo tomarlo?
4 ¿Es necesario ver a un médico?

TASK 4
Ask your teacher if he / she would mind checking over your work. Ask nicely! Ask him or her which (if any) areas need more revision (such as verbs or vocabulary). Don't forget to thank him / her!

En casa

checklist
What you need to know

Can you:

		Fine	Help!
1	say where you live and where it is?		
2	say whether you live in a house or a flat?		
3	describe your house or flat?		
4	name the rooms and say how many there are?		
5	find out about the rooms in somebody else's home?		
6	describe your room (contents, colour, size) and say where it is?		
7	describe different rooms and say what you do in each one?		
8	say if you have a garden and, if so, describe it?		
9	give information and find out about taking a bath or shower?		
10	give information and find out about daily routine?		
11	say what jobs you do around the house?		

At home

This topic is heavy on vocabulary. To ask questions about someone's home and to describe your own house, daily routine and jobs around the house, make sure you know set phrases which you can adapt by using different vocabulary.

Look at the Mind Maps on pages 102–5 to help you draw your own. There are one or two structures to bear in mind when you are describing your routine. Follow the signposts for helpful hints.

Help is at hand!

Notes/Options

1 ¿Dónde vives?

Vivo en Londres.
en las afueras de la ciudad — = in the outskirts of the city

en un pueblo en el campo — = in a village in the country

¿Dónde está Blackpool?

Está cerca del mar. — cerca de = near

en el sur / norte de Inglaterra — = in the south / north of England

este = east
oeste = west
norteste = north east
suroeste = south east

¿Cuál es tu dirección?
Es … — *Be prepared to spell out names.*

2 ¿Vives en una casa o en un piso?

Vivo en una casa.

3 ¿Cómo es tu casa? — ¿Cómo es? = what is it / he / she like?

Mi casa es grande. — *'Casa' also means home.*
pequeño/a = small
bastante = quite

Es un chalet. — chalet = detached house

Es de tres pisos.

¿Cómo es tu piso?

Es pequeño. Está en el primer piso.

piso / planta = floor	
primer piso = first floor	

See the Mind Map on page 102 for useful ways of remembering this vocabulary.

4/5 ¿Cuántas habitaciones tiene?

Tiene 8 habitaciones.

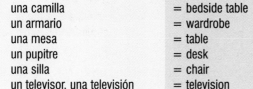

salón / cuarto de estar	= living room
el comedor	= dinning room
la cocina	= kitchen
el despacho	= study
mi dormitorio	dormitorio = bedroom
el dormitorio de mis padres	
el dormitorio de mi hermana	
el cuarto de baño / el baño	= bathroom
el aseo	= toilet

También hay un ático y un sótano.

Tiene un garaje doble.

el sótano = basement	
el garaje doble = double garage	
subterráneo	= underground

6 ¿Qué hay en tu dormitorio?

Hay una cama.

¿hay? = is / are there? hay = there is / are	
una cama = bed	
una camilla	= bedside table
un armario	= wardrobe
una mesa	= table
un pupitre	= desk
una silla	= chair
un televisor, una televisión	= television

¿De qué color es tu dormitorio?

Revise colours! See Mind Map on page 103.

Las paredes son blancas. las cortinas	las paredes = walls = curtains
La alfombra es gris.	la alfombra = carpet

Add an 's' or 'es' to the colour if you are describing more than one item e.g. **paredes y cortinas.**

¿Dónde está tu dormitorio?
Está en el segundo piso.

Está al lado del cuarto de baño

Está enfrente del dormitorio de mis padres.

el dormitorio de mis padres

al lado = next to	
enfrente = opposite	
= my parents' bedroom	

7 ¿Cómo son las habitaciones?

= What are the rooms like?	

Use the Mind Map on page 102 to help you describe the different rooms in your home.

¿Qué haces en el salón?
¿Qué haces?

Veo la televisión y escucho música.

= What do you do?	
veo = I watch escucho = I listen	

Make sure you know your verbs in the present tense. See pages 127 and 143–6.

8 ¿Tu casa tiene un jardín?

= Does your house have a garden?	

Sí, tiene un jardín bastante grande.

¿Cómo es tu jardín?

Tiene flores, árboles y un césped.

las flores = flowers los árboles = trees el césped = lawn	

¿Qué haces en el jardín?

9 ¿Puedo …?

¿Puedo bañarme / ducharme?

¿Dónde está el cuarto de baño?
¿Dónde está …?

Me hace falta necesito …

Me hace falta una toalla.
gel de ducha

= Can I…?	
= Can I have a bath / shower?	
= Where is …?	
I need …	
una toalla = towel = shower gel	

2

jabón	= soap
champú	= shampoo
pasta de dientes	= toothpaste
un cepillo de dientes	= toothbrush
La ducha no funciona.	= The shower isn't working.
grifo de agua caliente / fría	= hot / cold water tap
No hay papel higiénico.	= There is no toilet paper.

10 ¿Qué hora es? = What time is it?

¿A qué hora …? = At what time ?

Son las tres. / A las tres.

(A) Las tres y media.

(A) Las tres y cuarto.

(A) Las tres menos cuarto.

(A) Las tres y diez.

(A) Las tres menos diez.

You will need to use several reflexive verbs when describing your daily routine. Revise the forms explained on page 146.

LEVANTARSE	= to get up
me levanto	= I get up
te levantas	= you (tú) get up
se levanta	= he / she / you (usted) get/s up
nos levantamos	= we get up
os levantáis	= you (vosotros) get up
se levantan	= they / you (ustedes) get/s up

Don't confuse 'me' with 'yo': me = myself, yo = I.

You will also need to use verbs which are radical changing. See page 145.

DESPERTARSE	= to wake up
me despierto	= I wake up
te despiertas	= you (tú) wake up
se despierta	= he / she / you (usted) get/s up
nos despertamos	= we get up
os despertáis	= you (vosotros) get up
se despiertan	= they / you (ustedes) get up

Me acuesto a las diez.	acostarse = to go to bed
Me duermo a las diez y media.	dormirse = to go to sleep
¿Te vistes o te lavas primero?	vestirse = to get dressed lavarse = to get washed
¿A qué hora tomas el desayuno?	= At what time do you have breakfast?
Desayuno a las siete. Tomo el desayuno a las siete.	
Como a la una.	= I eat / lunch at one.
Meriendo a las cinco.	meriendo = I have tea
Ceno a las siete y media.	ceno = I have dinner
¿A qué hora sales de casa por la mañana?	por la mañana = in the morning

But note these differences: **mañana** = *tomorrow,* **mañana por la mañana** = *tomorrow morning.*

Salgo a las ocho y media.	salir = to leave / go out

Salir *is an irregular verb.*

Vuelvo a las cuatro menos cuarto.	volver = to return

11 ¿Qué haces para ayudar en casa? = What do you do to help at home?

Arreglo mi habitación.	= I tidy my room.
Saco la basura.	= I take out the rubbish.

Use the Mind Map on page 105 to help you describe household tasks.

Test yourself

Task 1

Read and record the Checklist questions on to a blank cassette. Try to answer the questions without looking at your notes. Time yourself and talk for a minute about your room mentioning size, contents and colours.

Going for a C?

Give as many details as possible, say when, where and how often you do things. Try to give simple opinions, such as Me gusta …/ No me gusta … por que es … Try to use the preterite tense (see pages 126 and 147) to talk about what you did last night, and the future tense to talk about what you will do at home tonight / tomorrow / at the weekend. In the role plays, be prepared to listen to the teacher – you will have one task in which you may have to respond to a question not given in the paper. During your preparation time, try to work out what the question could be. Use Time Markers.

Time Markers

normalmente	
generalmente	= normally
a veces / de vez en cuando	= sometimes
con frecuencia	
muchas veces	= sometimes
entonces	= then
después	= afterwards
el próximo	= the next
todos los días	= everyday
siempre	= always
nunca	= never
nunca jamás	= never ever

Task 2

Imagine you are staying with your Spanish pen-friend and his or her family. The mother wants to make sure that you are going to be comfortable. Use the prompts to ask for certain items and say what you need.

1 Pregunta.

2 Di lo que quieres.

3 Pregunta.

4 Di lo que quieres.

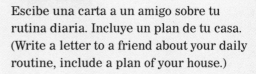

Task 3

Escribe una carta a un amigo sobre tu rutina diaria. Incluye un plan de tu casa. (Write a letter to a friend about your daily routine, include a plan of your house.)

Use the Notes/Options to help you. Remember Querido/a and Un saludo?

Label the plan with the rooms in the house, plus other features like gardens and garages.

Do you remember these?

desayuné	= I had breakfast	llegué	= I arrived
comí	= I had lunch / I ate	vi	= I watched
cené	= I had dinner	escuché	= I listened
me levanté	= I got up	leí	= I read
me acosté	= I went to bed	estudié	= I studied
dormí	= I slept	trabajé	= I worked
fui	= I went	ayudé	= I helped
salí	= I went out		

Answers

Task 2
1 ¿Dónde está el cuarto de baño?
2 ¿Me puedo duchar?
3 Necesito una toalla.
4 Me hace falta jabón.

Task 3
Ask a friend who is also learning Spanish to read through your work. Give yourself a point for each bit of information they can understand. More than eight points? Well done!

En casa

checklist
What you need to know

Can you:

	Fine	Help!
1 answer the questions on the Foundation Checklist on page 22?		

If you've ticked the Help! box, go back to the Foundation Notes/Options and revise!

2 discuss and express opinions about meals, meal times and eating habits?		
3 talk about your daily routine in the past and future?		
4 offer and ask to help around the house?		
5 say how you share and help with jobs around the house?		
6 say if you share a bedroom?		

At home

This topic comes up most frequently in Speaking and Listening papers so prepare to speak fluently about your eating habits, household tasks and daily routine. Try to include opinions without being prompted. Make sure you know the past and future tenses of the most commonly used verbs in this topic.

Help is at hand!

Notes/Options

1 *Only once you are really sure you are confident with the Foundation Checklist should you carry on with these Higher Notes/Options.*

2 ¿Cuál es tu plato preferido? — = What is your favourite dish?

Mi plato preferido es …

¿Cuál es tu bebida preferida? — bebida = drink

Mi bebida preferida es … / Prefiero beber … — beber = to drink

¿Qué no te gusta comer / beber?

No me gusta… / Odio …

Remember to add an 'n' on the end of me gusta *if you mention more than one item.*

No me gustan el pescado ni las hamburguesas.

If you need more help, look at Chapter 8.

Here are some useful phrases for expressing opinions about food.

Me encanta el queso.	= I love cheese.
Odio el queso.	= I hate cheese.
prefiero …	= I prefer
no me gusta(n) …	= I don't like
Me gusta(n) mucho …	= I really like …
No como carne de vaca / buey.	= I don't eat beef.

Es delicioso/a.	= It's delicious.
No tomo vino / alcohol.	= I don't drink wine / alcohol.
Es rico/a.	= It's delicious.
Está demasiado/a salado/a / dulce / picante.	= It's too salty / sweet / hot.
Huele bien.	= It smells good.
No me sienta bien.	= It gives me an upset stomach.
Es bueno para la salud.	= It's good for you.
Es malo para la salud.	= It's bad for you.
Engorda.	= It's fattening.

3 To talk about what you did in the past (last week, yesterday, last night, this morning, and so on) you need to use the preterite tense. See page 147 to help you revise the preterite tense.

¿Qué hiciste anoche?	= What did you do last night?
Anoche hice los deberes,	= I did my homework.
Fui a mi clase de piano.	= I went to my piano lesson.
Monté en bici.	= I rode my bike.
Cené pronto.	= I had dinner early.
Me acosté temprano.	= I went to bed early.

Have a look at the Mind Map on page 105.

When you hear these and similar time markers, use the preterite tense. Also use these markers when you talk about past actions.

Time Markers	
esta mañana	= this morning
anoche	= last night
ayer	= yesterday
el fin de semana pasado	= last weekend
el sábado pasado	= last Saturday
la semana pasada	= last week
el mes pasado	= last month
el año pasado	= last year
el verano pasado	= last summer

To talk about what you will do in the future (tonight, tomorrow, next week, and so on) use the future tense. See page 149 to help you revise this.

¿Qué harás esta tarde?	= What will you do this evening?
Llegaré a casa a las cuatro.	= I will arrive home at 4.00.
Merendaré.	= I will have a snack.
Veré un poco de televisión.	= I will watch a bit of TV.
Estudiaré.	= I will study.
No me acostaré tarde.	= I will not go to bed late.

When you hear these or similar time markers, use the future tense. Also use these markers when you talk about future actions.

Time Markers	
más tarde	= later
esta tarde	= tonight
mañana	= tomorrow
mañana por la mañana	= tomorrow morning
pasado mañana	= the day after tomorrow
el próximo fin de semana	= next weekend
el año que viene / próximo	= next year

4 ¿Le puedo ayudar? — *to an older person*

¿Te puedo ayudar / echar una mano? — *to a friend*

¿Puedo ayudar a poner la mesa?	= Can I help to lay the table?

Use the Mind Map on page 105 for phrases to describe housework.

5 ¿Qué tienes que hacer en casa?

Tengo que pasar la aspiradora.	= I have to do the vacuum cleaning.

Time Markers	
todos los días	= every day
un día sí y otro no	= every other day
una vez a la semana	= once a week
dos veces a la semana	= twice a week
los fines de semana	= at weekends
después de cenar	= after dinner

| Mi hermano tiene que fregar los platos. | = My brother has to do the washing up. |

Use phrases like these to give your opinion about who does what at home:

¡Es justo!	= It's fair
¡No es justo! / ¡No hay derecho!	= It's not fair!
¡Es desmasiado!	= It's too much!
¡No es bastante!	= It's not enough!
Hago más qué él / ella / ellos.	= I do more than him / her / them.
Hace/n más que yo.	= He / she / they do more than me.
En mi opinión… es / son perezoso/a(s).	= he / she / they are lazy.
debería/n ayudar más.	= he / she / they should help more.
debería/n sacar la basura más amenudo.	= he / she / they should take out the rubbish more often.

See the Mind Map on rooms and colours on page 103.

6 | ¿Compartes tu dormitorio / habitación? | = Do you share your bedroom / room? |
| No, tengo mi propio dormitorio. | = No, I have my own room. |
| Sí, comparto mi dormitorio con mi hermana. | comparto = I share |

Going for an A?

Revise the conditional tense (see page 149) then try the Test Yourself tasks.

Test yourself

Task 1

Describe tu dormitorio ideal. (100/120 palabras) (Describe your ideal room.) Use these phrases to help you:

me gustaría / quisiera	= I would like
tener	= to have
comprar	= to buy
decorar	= to decorate
habría	= there would be
sería	= it would be

Try to add reasons for why you would like to have something. Talk about colour, size and so on. Ask your teacher if he / she would mind checking your work. Remember to thank him / her!

Task 2

Listen to the cassette (Side 1, Chapter 2) and fill in this grid.

Escribe VERDAD o MENTIRA para cada una de estas frases:

AFIRMACION	¿VERDAD O MENTIRA?
1 Teresa empezó a beber cuando tenía once años.	
2 Una amiga bebió una copita de anís.	
3 Después Teresa bebió anís con sus padres.	
4 Carlos nunca ha bebido alcohol.	
5 Carlos no bebe más.	

Answers

TASK 2
1 Verdad
2 Mentira
3 Mentira
4 Mentira
5 Verdad

3

En mi tiempo libre

In my spare time

This topic is fun to learn because it's all about your personal interests. You can talk about whatever or whoever you devote your spare time to and give as many opinions about that activity or person as you like. Adapt the models in the Notes/Options to prepare for writing and speaking about your likes and dislikes.

Help is at hand!

Notes/Options

1 ¿Qué haces en tu tiempo libre?

Look at the Mind Map on page 106.

Salgo con mis amigos y monto en bicicleta.

Juego al tenis / fútbol.

Practico la natación / la gimnasia.

Leo, me gustan libros de ciencia ficción.

revistas = magazines
periódicos = newspapers
tebeos = comics

Escucho música.

Juego con mi ordenador.

el ordenador = computer

Toco la guitarra.

Remember **toco** *and* **juego** *both mean I play, but* **toco** *is for instruments and* **juego** *is for sports and games.*

2 ¿Desde cuándo haces eso?

= How long have you been doing that?

Desde hace un año / seis meses.

= For a year / six months.

3 Me gusta jugar al fútbol porque es emocionante.

emocionante = exciting

Mi equipo preferido es Liverpool.

equipo = team

Mi futbolista preferido es Ryan Giggs.

futbolista = footballer

checklist
What you need to know

Can you:

	Fine	Help!
1 understand and give details about how you like to spend your spare time (hobbies, sports, clubs, music, TV and going out)?		
2 say how long you have been following your interests?		
3 say why you like to do certain things?		
4 ask others what they do in their spare time?		
5 ask what a friend would like to do?		
6 ask for and give information about when activities start and finish?		
7 arrange to meet at a certain time and place and check and change arrangements?		
8 buy tickets for sports and leisure activities such as sports centres and cinemas?		
9 apologise for being late?		
10 say what kinds of films and TV programmes you watch?		
11 say how much pocket money you get and what you spend it on?		
12 say what there is to do in the area where you live?		
13 say what you did last weekend?		
14 say what you plan to do next weekend?		

Pertenezco al equipo de mi colegio.	pertenezco = I belong to
Nos entrenamos todos los fines de semana.	= We train every weekend.
¿Eres deportivo/a?	= Are you sporty?
No, no me gusta el deporte.	
No juego bien y me canso.	me canso = I get tired
¿Te gusta tocar la guitarra?	
¿Qué tipo de música te gusta?	
Me gusta la música pop / rock / reggae / clásica. Es romántica / emocionante / dramática. Es música marchosa.	= It is dance music.
¿Cuál es tu grupo / cantante preferido?	el / la cantante = singer
Mi grupo preferido es Oasis. Son fantásticos.	
4 ¿Qué haces en tu tiempo libre?	
¿Qué te gusta hacer en tu tiempo libre?	
5 ¿Qué te gustaría hacer hoy / esta tarde / mañana?	= What would you like to do today / this afternoon, evening / tomorrow?

Do you remember?

To ask someone if they would like to do something, you can either use ¿Quieres? or ¿Te gustaría? + the verb in the infinitive.

¿Te gustaría / Quieres…	= Would you like / Do you want …
… salir?	= … to go out?
… jugar al baloncesto?	= … to play basketball?
… tomar algo?	= … to have a drink?
… dar una vuelta?	= … to go for a walk?
… ir de compras?	= … to go shopping?

To ask someone if they would like to go somewhere, you can either use ¿Te gustaría? or ¿Quieres + ir + the place?

¿Quieres / Te gustaría ir …	
a la discoteca?	
a la piscina?	
a la hamburguesería?	
a la bolera?	
al parque de atracciones?	

6 ¿A qué hora empieza la película?	= What time does the film start?
el concierto	= concert
el espectáculo	= show
el partido	= the match
La película empieza a las 8h00.	
El partido termina a las 7h30.	

Remember that starting and finishing times may need the 24-hour clock, such as 7.30 pm = 19h.

7 ¿Quieres salir a cenar?	= Do you want to go out to dinner?
Bueno, estoy libre.	= OK, I'm free.
¿A qué hora nos encontramos?	= What time shall we meet?
¿Nos encontramos a las 6h00?	= Shall we meet at 6 o'clock?

es demasiado pronto / temprano	= that's too early
es demasiado tarde	= that's too late
de acuerdo	= that's fine
no puedo	= I can't
lo siento	= I'm sorry
¿Está bien? / ¿Te parece bien?	= Is that OK?

8 Vamos al cine.

Quisiera una entrada para la sesión de las 8h00. = I'd like a seat for the 8 o'clock show.

¿Cuánto vale la entrada? = How much is it to get in?

9 Lo siento. Llego tarde. = I'm sorry I'm late.

Remember that you can use lo siento *or* perdón *to say you are sorry.*

10 ¿Ves mucha televisión? = Do you watch a lot of TV?

Si, veo la tele todas las tardes.

¿Qué tipo de programas prefieres?

See the Mind Map on page 107.

¿Cuál es tu programa preferido?

Mi programa preferido es Brookside porque es interesante.

¿Vas a menudo al cine? a menudo = often

Voy al cine una vez el mes. una vez al mes = once a month

un par de veces = a couple of times

No voy nunca. = I never go.

¿Cuál fue la última película que viste? = What was the last film you saw?

¿Qué te pareció? = What did you think of it?

¿Te gustó? = Did you like it?

11 ¿Te dan dinero tus padres? = Do you get pocket money?

Me dan 5 libras a la semana. a la semana = a week

¿En qué te lo gastas? = What do you spend it on?

¿En qué te gastas el dinero / la paga? la paga = pocket money

Me lo gasto en ropa y cosméticos. = I spend it on clothes and make up.

Compro videojuegos y caramelos. = I buy video games and sweets.

salir con los amigos = to go out with friends

comprar una bici de montaña = to buy a mountain bike

12 ¿Qué hay para jóvenes en tu barrio? = What is there to do for young people in your area?

¿Qué hay de interés en tu pueblo? = What's of interest in your town?

Hay un estadio, campos de tenis y un centro comercial. = There is a stadium, tennis courts and a shopping centre.

How is your memory?

Se puede + infinitive = you can / one can + activity
Se puede + ir de paseo
bailar
ver un partido
jugar al tenis de mesa

13 ¿Qué hiciste el fin de semana pasado? = What did you do last weekend?

Revise the preterite tense so that you can talk about what you did. See pages 126 and 147.

Time Markers	
el sábado pasado	= last Saturday
anoche	= last night
ayer por la tarde	= yesterday afternoon
la semana pasada	= last week

Here are some useful phrases about activities in the preterite tense.

fui de compras	= I went shopping
jugé al baloncesto	= I played basketball
salí con mis amigos	= I went out with my friends
ví una película	= I watched a film
toqué el saxofón	= I played the saxophone
escuché música	= I listened to music
monté en bicicleta	= I rode my bike
lo pasé bien	= I had a good time
me divertí	= I enjoyed myself

Look at the Mind Maps on pages 106–109, and 112 for extra help.

14 ¿Qué vas a hacer este fin de semana?   = What are you going to do this weekend?

There are two ways to talk about your future plans. You can use voy + infinitive or the full future tense.

Voy + infinitive	
voy a visitar a mis abuelos	= I'm going to visit my grandparents
voy a estudiar	= I'm going to study
voy a ir a la piscina	= I'm going to the swimming-pool
lo voy a pasar bien	= I'm going to have a good time
me voy a divertir	= I'm going to enjoy myself

To revise the future tense see pages 128 and 149.

iré	= I will go
jugaré	= I will play (game / sport)
saldré	= I will go out
veré	= I will watch
tocaré	= I will play (music / instrument)
escucharé	= I will listen
montaré	= I will ride
lo pasaré bien	= I will have a good time
me divertiré	= I will enjoy myself

Time Markers	
esta tarde	= this afternoon
mañana	= tomorrow
mañana por la tarde	= tomorrow afternoon
este fin de semana	= this weekend
el fin de semana próximo	= next weekend
la semana que viene	= next week

Test yourself

Task 1

Listen to Side 1, Chapter 3, Foundation. Play the exercise twice.

Teresa te ha mandado un cassette en el que menciona cinco (5) de sus hobbys. ¿Cuáles son?

Pon una señal ✔ al lado de los cinco (5) hobbys.

Ejemplo.

 ☑

Ahora mira los dibujos.

Ahora escucha a Teresa.

Task 2

Time yourself and talk for at least 15 seconds on each of the following topics:

el deporte   la música
la televisión   esta tarde
el cine
el fin de semana pasado
el fin de semana que viene

Use written cheats to help you until you feel that you can talk without hesitating. Can you manage 30 seconds on any of them? ¡Enhorabuena!

Task 3

Read the following letter from a Spanish pen-pal and mark whether the following statements are true or false.

¡Hola!

Me llamo Gabriel. Tengo 15 años y vivo en Vitoria. Me gustan mucho los deportes. Juego al tenis dos veces a la semana y practico el atletismo. Desde hace un año soy miembro del equipo de baloncesto de mi instituto. Somos campeones regionales. Nos entrenamos dos veces a la semana. También me gusta el fútbol. Voy a ver los partido de mi equipo provincial en el estadio del pueblo con mis amigos. Lo pasamos muy bien. ¿Eres deportivo?

En mi tiempo libre me gusta escuchar música. Me encanta el rock, especialmente el heavy metal. Mi grupo preferido es Metálica, son fantásticos. ¿Qué tipo de música te gusta?

No me gusta ver la televisión, es aburrido. Prefiero ir al cine. Voy todas las semanas. Me gustan las películas de acción. La semana pasada fui a ver Chain Reaction con Keanu Reeves que es mi actor preferido. Me gustó mucho, es una película muy inteligente. ¿Vas a menudo al cine?

¿Qué haces en tu tiempo libre? ¿Cómo es un fin de semana típico para ti?

		Cierto	Falso
1	Gabriel pertenece a un equipo de baloncesto.	☐	☐
2	Su equipo se entrena en el estadio del pueblo.	☐	☐
3	Se divierte cuando ve los partidos de fútbol.	☐	☐
4	No le gusta la música.	☐	☐
5	Prefiere la televisión al cine.	☐	☐
6	Va a menudo al cine.	☐	☐
7	Va a ver Chain Reaction este fin de semana.	☐	☐
8	Le gusta Keanu Reeves porque es inteligente.	☐	☐

Now try to correct the statements that were false.

Task 4

Escribe una carta a un amigo español (60 a 80 palabras). Describe lo que haces en tu tiempo libre.

Use the letter in Task 3 as a model for your own letter. Use time marker words such as normalmente, a veces and a menudo. Ask questions in your letter. The examiner will be marking you on how accurately (correctly) you can communicate. Check that you can communicate what you want to say by looking at the Mind Maps. Make sure you understand a question before you start to answer it. Use a dictionary to check key words. Don't ignore time markers such as normalmente, pasado or próximo as they will indicate whether you should use the present, past or future tenses.

Answers

TASK 1
1, 5, 6, 10

TASK 3
1 Cierto   3 Cierto   5 Falso   7 Cierto
2 Falso   4 Falso   6 Falso   8 Falso

1 Gabriel pertenece a un equipo de baloncesto.
2 Su equipo no se entrena en el estadio.
4 Le encanta la música.
5 Prefiere el cine a la televisión.
6 Fue a va a ver Chain Reaction el fin de semana pasada.
8 Le gustó porque es una película inteligente.

checklist

What you need to know

Can you:

	Fine	Help!
1 answer the questions on the Foundation Checklist on page 29?		

If you've ticked the Help! box, go back to the Foundation Notes/Options and revise!

2 ask if an activity is available?		
3 discuss times of sessions and performances?		
4 say why you prefer to do something?		
5 ask if a play or film was good?		
6 discuss and give an opinion about a film, TV programme or activity?		
7 tell someone what a film or play was about?		
8 say what you would like to do if you had the money and the time?		

In my spare time

You must be able to give opinions and reasons for your opinions at this level. Make sure you know the phrases for expressing likes and dislikes by checking the Mind Maps on pages 108 and 112 before you go any further. You should also be prepared to give a simple description of the plot of a film or play, you can do it in the present tense but if you want to impress the examiner you must use the past tenses (preterite and imperfect).

To describe what you would do if you, say, won the lottery you need to use the conditional and the subjunctive. It is easiest to do this by learning set phrases by heart. Use the Mind Maps on pages 106–112 to help you draw a personalised Mind Map to describe your leisure activities.

Help is at hand!

Notes/Options

1 *Only once you are really sure you are confident with the Foundation Checklist should you carry on with these Higher Notes/Options.*

2 ¿Hay una discoteca por aquí / en tu barrio?	= Is there a disco around here / in your area?
¿Se puede montar a caballo por aquí?	= Can you go horse-riding around here?
¿Qué ponen en el cine esta semana?	= What's on at the cinema this week?
¿Qué hay en la tele esta noche?	= What's on TV tonight?
¿Es posible alquilar bicicletas?	= Is it possible to hire bicycles?
¿Podemos ir de excursión?	= Can we go on a trip?
¿Tienes una guía de televisión?	= Do you have a TV guide?
3 ¿Cuántas sesiones hay?	= How many performances / showings are there?

¿A qué hora es la sesión de la tarde? = What time is the afternoon / evening performance?

¿Es sesión continua? = Is it a continuous performance?

¿A qué hora empieza el concierto esta tarde? = What time does this evening's concert begin?

¿A qué hora termina? = What time does it finish?

4 ¿Qué prefieres hacer? = What do you prefer to do?

Prefiero ir de paseo porque hace buen tiempo. = I prefer to go for a walk because the weather is good.

No quiero salir porque hay fútbol en la tele. = I don't want to go out because there is football on TV.

Prefiero quedarme en casa porque estoy cansado/a. = I prefer to stay in because I'm tired.

5 ¿Qué te pareció la película?

¿Era bueno el concierto?

¿Te gustó el programa?

¿Qué tal el teatro?

6

Me parece que … =	It seems to me …
es bueno para la salud	es demasiado caro
es malo para la salud	es muy útil
es muy barato	es una pérdida de tiempo

Creo que … =	I believe …
es muy divertido	cansa mucho
es muy aburrido	es típico
es emocionante	es cruel

Pienso que … =	I think …
es fascinante	es tonto
es estúpido	es relajante
es cómico	es estresante
es deprimente	es genial
es impresionante	es ridículo

Remember: if you want to emphasise something in Spanish you add particular endings to the adjectives.

bueno/a(s)	buenísimo/a(s)
malo/a(s)	malísimo/a(s)
rico/a(s)	riquísimo/a(s)
peligroso/a(s)	peligrosísimo/a(s)

7 ¿De qué trataba la obra de teatro? = What was the play about?

¿Qué pasó en la película? = What happened in the play?

Revise your preterite and imperfect tenses. See page 147.

Trataba de … = It was about …

Learn the differences between these three verbs	
era	= he / she it was
Era durante la guerra.	= It was during the war.
Era un soldado.	= He was a soldier.
fue	= he / she / it was
Fue a Francia.	= He went to France.
Fue herido.	= He was wounded.
estaba	= he / she / it was
Estaba muy enfermo.	= He was very ill.
Estaba en el hospital.	= He was in hospital.

8 ¿Qué harías si tuvieras mucho dinero y tiempo libre?

Si tuviera mucho dinero … = If I had lots of money …

Have a look at page 149 to revise more on the conditional tense.

iría	= I would go
Iría de vacaciónes a Sudamérica.	= I would go on holiday to South America.
compraría	= I would buy
Compraría una moto.	= I would buy a motorbike.
jugaría	= I would play
Jugaría mucho al tenis.	= I would play a lot of tennis.
haría	= I would do
Haría mucho deporte.	= I would do lots of sport.
tendría	= I would have
Tendría una casa en la Costa Brava.	= I would have a house on the Costa Brava.

Going for an A?

Be ready to give your opinion and to say why you have that opinion!

Test yourself

Task 1

Listen to Side 1, Chapter 3, Higher.
Play the cassette twice.

Escucha esta entrevista con unos jóvenes
españoles sobre el ocio. Rellena las casillas,
escribiendo el nombre de cada uno de los jóvenes
al lado de su descripción.

Se llaman:
Catalina, Andrés, Maritere, Dolores, Guillermo

		¿Quién es?
1	Esta persona piensa que el fútbol es ahora un deporte muy aburrido en España.	
2	A esta persona no le gustan nada los deportes de nieve, porque cree que son peligrosos.	
3	Lo único que le gusta a esta persona es quedarse en casa con un buen libro.	
4	Esta persona no puede decidir si le encanta más el cine o el teatro.	
5	Esta persona no tiene derecho a expresar sus opiniones porque tiene unos padres muy estrictos.	

Task 2

Use the box to prepare a talk (1½ – 2 mins).

Mis actividades			
Por la tarde	El fin de semana		
¿Cuándo?	¿Cómo?	¿Dónde?	¿Con quién?
¿Preferencias?	¿Por qué?		

TASK 1

1 Guillermo **2** Andrés, **3** Maritere, **4** Dolores, **5** Catalina

Answers

Task 3

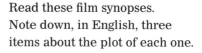

Read these film synopses.
Note down, in English, three
items about the plot of each one.

La película del mes
BARB WIRE
La mayoría de los cachorros de estrella se han consagrado con
películas de acción: Christian Slater en *Alarma Nuclear*, Keanu
Reeves en *Speed*…. Ahora Winona Ryder protagonizará la nueva
entrega de *Alien* y, en esta ocasión, Pamela es una *superchica* que,
en un futuro devastador, es capaz de enfrentarse a todo tipo de
malvados, enfundada en cuero negro de pies a cabeza y montada
en su moto de alta cilindrada. Otra de las sorpresas de la cinta es la
presencia de Jack Noiseworthy – acuérdate, el bombón del vídeo
de Bon Jovi *Always* –, interpretando al hermano de Pamela.

No te la pierdas
UN LOCO A DOMICILIO
Jim Carrey suspira por un papel dramático; pero mientras, continúa
sobreactuando como un poseso en películas rompetaquillas e
inocuas como ésta. Aquí es un pesadísimo instalador de televisión
por cable, que se cuela en la vida de Mathew Broderick obsesionado
por convertirse en su amigo. Y lo único que consigue es ahuyentar a
sus colegas, parientes y posibles novias y, convertirle en alguien tan
enloquecido como él. Una película que sólo soportarán los que sean
capaces de seguir el ritmo al extragesticulante Carrey. No hay
términos medios: O le odias, o le amas.

Now try to write your own synopsis of a film you
have seen recently.

Note that the synopses you have just read are in
the present tense because they are written for
readers who have not yet seen the film. However,
you can use the present or past tense. But
remember – the examiner is looking to see if you
can use past tenses!

Task 4

Escribe un artículo (120 palabras) sobre
lo que hay para jóvenes en tu pueblo o
ciudad. Use this plan to help you.

En mi opinión …

1 Los servicios
Polideportivo, centro comercial,
cine, estadio, club de jóvenes

2 Tus opiniones

¿Hay bastante que hacer?

5 ¿Cómo se podrían
mejorar los servicios para
jóvenes?

El tiempo libre

3 Mis pasatiempos
por las tardes
los fines de semana.

4 Actividades deportivas

¿Qué se puede hacer?

4

De vacaciones

Booking in

This topic is heavy on language for making transactions. This means it will probably come up in the speaking and listening sections of the exam. Use the Notes/Options and Mind Maps (pages 113 and 114) to familiarise yourself with the language you will need. Remember that you may have to write a letter booking into a hotel or a campsite so learn the set phrases given in this chapter for writing a letter.

Help is at hand!

Notes/Options

En el hotel

1 He reservado dos habitaciones para mi familia.

= I've reserved two rooms for my family.

Telefoné para hacer una reserva.

= I phoned to make a reservation.

Escribí para reservar unas habitaciones.

= I wrote to reserve some rooms.

¿Necesita ver mi pasaporte?

= Do you need to see my passport?

Check the Mind Map on page 113.

2 ¿Tiene habitaciones libres para esta noche?

= Do you have any rooms for tonight?

¿Tiene libre una habitación doble?

= Do you have a double room?

¿Hay habitaciones individuales?

= Are there any single rooms?

3 Quisiera una habitación para mí.

= I would like a room for myself.

… para mis padres.

= … for my parents.

… para mis compañeros.

= … for my friends.

Es por una noche.

= It's for one night.

Quisiera una habitación con baño.

= I'd like a room with a bathroom.

… con vistas al mar.

= … with a view of the sea.

checklist
What you need to know

Can you:

		Fine	Help!
At a hotel			
1	check in?	●	●
2	ask if rooms are available?	●	●
3	say what accommodation you need?	●	●
4	ask the cost of a room?	●	●
5	ask to see the rooms?	●	●
6	ask about facilities?	●	●
7	ask about keys?	●	●
8	ask about meals?	●	●
9	say you want to check out?	●	●
10	ask if there are any hostel beds available?	●	●
11	say how many of you there are?	●	●
12	ask for a sleeping bag?	●	●
13	ask where the facilities are?	●	●
14	ask if there are any jobs?	●	●
15	understand hostel rules?	●	●
16	ask for space for a tent?	●	●
17	ask about campsite facilities?	●	●
18	ask about campsite rules?	●	●
General			
19	make a complaint	●	●
20	ask for details about places to visit?	●	●

4

… con cama matrimonial. = … with a double bed.

… con camas individuales. = … with single beds.

4 ¿Cuánto es la habitación por noche? = How much is a room per night?

¡Es demasiado cara! = It is too expensive.

¿Está incluido el desayuno? = Is breakfast included?

5 ¿Es posible ver la habitación? = Can I see the room?

La cojo. = I'll take it.

Lo siento. No la quiero. = I don't want it.

6 ¿El hotel tiene un parking? = Is there a hotel car park?

¿Hay un secador en la habitación? = Is there a hairdryer in the room?

7 ¿Me puede dar la llave? = Can you give me the key?

¿Cuál es el número de la habitación? = What is the room number?

Es el 23 en el segundo piso. = It's number 23 on the second floor.

¿A qué hora cierra el hotel? = What time does the hotel close?

¿Me puede dar una llave para la puerta principal? = Can you give me a front door key?

8 ¿A qué hora se sirve el desayuno? = What time is breakfast?

Quisiera pensión completa. = I would like full board.

¿Cuánto es la media pensión? = How much is half board?

9 Quisiera pagar la cuenta, por favor. = I'd like to pay the bill, please.

¿Acepta tarjetas de crédito? = Do you take credit cards?

En el albergue juvenil
10 ¿Tiene una cama libre? = Do you have any beds available?

11 Estoy sólo/a. = I'm on my own.

¿Quiere ver mi tarjeta de afiliación? = Do you want to see my membership card?

¿Necesito rellenar esta ficha? = Do I have to fill in this form?

12 Quisiera alquilar un saco de dormir. = I'd like to hire a sleeping bag.

13 ¿Dónde están las duchas? = Where are the showers?

… los aseos? = … the toilets?

14 ¿Hay que hacer alguna tarea? = Are there any jobs to do?

Check the Mind Map on page 114 for further useful phrases you would need in a youth hostel.

15 Las normas

PROHIBIDO COMER EN LOS DORMITORIOS

IT IS FORBIDDEN TO EAT IN THE DORMITORIES

SE PROHIBE FREGAR Y LAVAR ROPA EN LOS LAVABOS

WASHING DISHES AND CLOTHES IS NOT PERMITTED IN THE HAND-BASINS

SE RUEGA SILENCIO DESPUES DE LAS 23H

SILENCE IS REQUESTED AFTER 11 PM

ALBERGUE CERRADO A LAS 22H 30.

HOSTEL CLOSED AT 10.30 PM

En el camping

16 ¿Hay sitio para una tienda?   = Is there room for a tent?

Lo siento, está completo.   = I'm sorry, we are full.

¿Para cuántas personas?   = For how many people?

Somos cinco, dos adultos y tres niños.   = There are five of us, two adults and three children.

¿Para cuántos días?   = For how many days?

Para una semana.   = For a week.

Quisiera un sitio a la sombra.   = I'd like a pitch in the shade.

… debajo de los árboles.   = … under the trees.

Check the Mind Map on page 114 to make sure you know the vocabulary for campsite facilities.

17 ¿Hay una lavandería?   = Is there a launderette?

18 ¿Se pueden encender lumbres?   = Can you light a fire?

¿Es posible hacer una barbacoa?   = Is it possible to have a barbecue?

19 ¡Cuando las cosas van mal …!   When things go wrong …!

No hay toallas.   = There are no towels.

… agua calliente.   = … hot water.

El ascensor no funciona.   = The lift doesn't work.

Hay demasiado ruido.   = There is too much noise.

20 See Chapter 3, Checklist 12 on page 31.

Going for a C?

Learn how to write a letter booking accommodation. Learn the highlighted phrases first.

The letter can be adapted by changing details as necessary. It can also be used as the basis for booking into a campsite or youth hostel. To book places at a youth hostel for two boys and two girls, you need to say: Quisiera reservar **plazas** / **camas** para **dos chicos y dos chicas**.

Londres, 2 de abril

Muy señor mío:[1]

¿Me puede decir si tiene[2] habitaciones libres por quince días **apartir** del día 2 de agosto **hasta** el 17[3]?

Quisiera[4] una habitación doble con cama matrimonial y con baño y otra con ducha con dos camas individuales y , **si es posible**[5], con vistas al mar.

Le ruego me confirme[6] la reserva de las habitaciones **a su más pronta conveniencia**[7].

Le ruego tambien que **me mande**[8] un folleto sobre el hotel[9] y que me informe sobre los precios[10] y el depósito que debo remitirle[11].

Le saluda atentamente[12],

Louis Jordan

[1] Dear Sir
[2] Can you tell me if you have …
[3] from (date) to (date)
[4] I would like …
[5] If possible
[6] Please confirm …
[7] At your earliest convenience
[8] Please send me …
[9] A brochure about the hotel
[10] Inform me about your prices
[11] the deposit I should send
[12] Yours faithfully

4

Test yourself

Task 1

Lee la lista de servicios. ¿Cuáles de los servicios en la lista ofrece el camping? Marca (✔) en las casillas apropiadas.

CARLOS III   2.ª C ☎ 742001
Situado en: Ctra. Valencia-Barcelona, Km. 160
Abierto del 1 de Junio al 30 de Setiembre.

Distancia a la playa: 6 m.   Capacidad: 298 personas.

Precio por dia: +I.V.A.

		Ptas.			Ptas.
parcela	☐	750	coche		375
persona		375	caravana		375
niño		325	motocicleta		325
tienda ind.	⚐	325	coche cama		700
tienda fam.	⚐	375	autocar		800

El precio de la parcela incluye coche y tienda o coche y caravana.

1	Arboles	☐
2	Correos	☐
3	Admisión de animales de compañia	☐
4	Mini golf	☐
5	Duchas de agua caliente	☐
6	Parque infantil	☐
7	Pesca	☐
8	Consulta médica	☐
9	Enchufes eléctricos	☐
10	Biblioteca	☐
11	Pista de tenis	☐

Task 2

Try this role play.
You are booking into a youth hostel.

1 Pregunta.

2 Di para quiénes son las reservas.

3 Di lo que quieres.

4 Pregunta.

Task 3

Listen to the cassette (Side 1, Chapter 4, Foundation). Play the cassette twice.

Escucha la conversación entre un cliente y una recepcionista en un hotel. ¿Qué tipo de reserva quiere hacer el cliente? Completa las frases y contesta las preguntas rellenando los espacios en blanco en español.

1 Número de habitaciones con camas individuales: …………

2 Número de habitaciones con camas matrimoniales: …………

3 ¿Baño o ducha? ………………

4 ¿Para cuántas noches? …………

5 ¿Desayuno o media pensión? ………………

6 ¿Con vista de qué? ………………..

7 Servicios que ofrece el hotel: ………………

8 Situación del hotel: ……………

9 Piscina abierta de …..h a ……….h …………

10 El hotel hay: ……………

Task 4

Read this reply to a letter making a hotel booking.

Hotel Miramar
Paseo de las delicias, 23, Valencia

Estimado señor:[1]

Acusamos recibo de su atenta carta[2] de fecha 8 de mayo y **nos es grato informarle**[3] que le hemos reservado una habitación doble con cuarto de baño para ocho días a partir del 22 de agosto.

Lamentamos tener que decirle[4] que para esa fecha **no tenemos disponible ninguna habitación exterior**[5] con vista al mar, **por lo que**[6] le hemos reservado una interior.

Adjunto le enviamos[7] un folleto descriptivo del hotel con un plano de localización.

Le saludamos muy atentamente[8] y **quedamos a su disposición.**[9]

Lucía Pérez

Gerente[10]

---

[1] Dear Sir

[2] We have received your letter …

[3] We are pleased to inform you …

[4] We regret to inform you …

[5] We have no outside rooms available

[6] Consequently

[7] We enclose …

[8] Yours sincerely

[9] We are at your disposal

[10] Manager

Although you might not have to use the phrases in a business letter at this level, make sure you recognise them, especially:

No tenemos disponible ninguna habitación.	= We have no rooms available.

Remember that business letters in Spanish are very formal. Try writing the booking letter to which the hotel is replying. Check back to the booking letter on page 39 to see if you have written the highlighted phrases correctly.

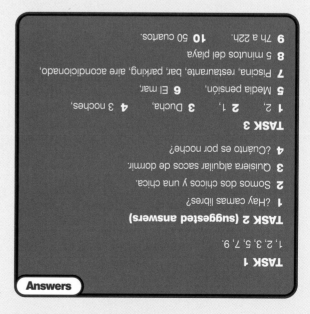

Answers

TASK 1

1, 2, 3, 5, 7, 9.

TASK 2 (suggested answers)

1 ¿Hay camas libres?

2 Somos dos chicos y una chica.

3 Quisiera alquilar sacos de dormir.

4 ¿Cuánto es por noche?

TASK 3

1 2, **2** 1, **3** Ducha, **4** 3 noches, **5** Media pensión, **6** El mar, **7** Piscina, restaurante, bar, parking, aire acondicionado, **8** 5 minutos del playa, **9** 7h a 22h, **10** 50 cuartos.

Look back at the Checklist.

De vacaciones

checklist
What you need to know

Can you:

	Fine	Help!
1 answer the questions on the Foundation Checklist on page 37?	●	●

If you've ticked any of the Help! boxes go back to the Foundation Notes/Options to revise.

At a hotel

2 cope with unexpected situations, such as mistaken identity, incorrect reservation details, loosing keys, accidents in the hotel room?	●	●
3 make more detailed complaints, such as lack of facilities / too much noise?	●	●
4 write a letter of complaint to a hotel explaining the problem?	●	●

Booking in

The difference between Foundation and Higher Levels in this topic is that for this level you need to be able to make complaints in detail. You should be able to complain in writing as well as verbally, and to make complaints about past events. If you need help look out for the helpful hints and refer to the Mind Maps on pages 113 and 114.

Help is at hand!

Notes/Options

1 *Only once you are really sure you are confident with the Foundation Checklist should you carry on with these Higher Notes/Options.*

2

Está equivocado/a. No soy la señorita Smith, soy … la señorita Jones.	= You have made a mistake. I'm not Miss … Smith, I'm Miss Jones.
Reservé una habitación la semana pasada.	= I reserved a room last week.
Pedí una habitación con terraza.	= I asked for a room with a balcony.
Quería sólo una habitación.	= I only wanted one room.
Le escribí, aquí tengo su carta de confirmación.	= I wrote to you, here is my letter of confirmation.
Le mandé un fax.	= I sent you a fax.
Ya he pagado un depósito.	= I have already paid a deposit.
Hay un error en la cuenta.	= There is a mistake on the bill.

Revise the preterite tense.
See pages 126 and 147.

RESERVAR	= to reserve
he reservado	= I have reserved
has reservado	= you (tú) have reserved
ha reservado	= he / she / you (usted) have reserved
hemos reservado	= we have reserved
habéis reservado	= you (vosotros) have reserved
han reservado	= they / you (ustedes) have reserved

PERDER	= to lose
he perdido	= I have lost
has perdido	= you (tú) have lost
ha perdido	= he / she / you (usted) have lost
hemos perdido	= we have lost
habéis perdido	= you (vosotros) have lost
han perdido	= they / you (ustedes) have lost

3

Tengo una queja.	= I have a complaint.
No puedo dormir. Hay demasiado ruido.	= I can't sleep. There is too much noise.
No habían mantas en la habitación.	= There were no blankets in the room.
El agua está frío.	= The water is cold.
El servicio era muy lento.	= The service was slow.
La recepcionista no era cortés.	= The receptionist was not polite.
La comida estaba fría.	= The food was cold.
hacer una reclamación	= to ask for a refund

Going for an A?

A letter of complaint

York, el 2 de junio

Gerente
Hotel Fortuna

Estimada Sra:

Me dirijo atentamente a Usted[1] para manifestarle mi disconformidad[2] con el servicio que me fue prestado[3] en el hotel a su cargo durante mi estancia la noche del 21 de mayo.

Deseo expresarle[4] que el mal servicio al que me refiero fue[5] que la televisión no funcionaba. Llamé tres veces a la recepción pero no subieron a repararla.

Al mismo tiempo[6] pasé mala noche a cuasa del ruido de la discoteca del hotel que no acabó hasta las tres de la madrugada. Además, el cuarto de baño estaba sucio y no habían suficientes toallas.

Creo que un hotel de tres estrellas debería ofrecer un mejor servicio.[7]

Le sugiero que ponga más atención al personal que trabaja en el hotel.[8] Espero que no tarde en reembolsarme el dinero que pagué.[9]

La saluda atentamente,

Tracy Buxton

[1] I am writing …

[2] … to complain …

[3] … about the service that I received

[4] I should like to inform you …

[5] … that the poor service to which I am refering was …

[6] At the same time …

[7] I think a 3-star hotel should offer better service.

[8] I suggest that more attention is paid to the staff employed at the hotel.

[9] I hope you will refund the cost of my stay as soon as possible.

4 Me dirijo a Vd. para quejarme enérgicamente.

= I am writing to you to make a strong complaint.

Espero que haga las averiguaciones correspondientes.

= I hope you make the necessary investigations.

¿Ruego que pueda reembolsarme el dinero?

= Can you please repay my costs?

Sugiero que ponga más atención.

= I suggest you pay more attention.

Check that you know when to use the subjunctive. See page 149.

If you find the subjunctive difficult, make sure you know the set phrases above.

Present	Imperfect	Preterite
Hay	*Había*	*Hubo*
No hay luz. =	No había mantas. =	Hubo tormenta. =
There is no light.	There were no blankets.	There was a storm.
Está	*Estaba*	*Estuvo*
La sopa está fría. = The soup is cold.	Las sábanas estaban sucias. = The sheets were dirty.	Estuve una noche. = I was there one night.
Es	*Era*	*Fue*
Es demasiado pequeño. = It is too small.	Era muy incómodo. = It was uncomfortable.	Fue un desastre. = It was a disaster.

Make sure you know when to use these tenses by checking pages 126, 127 and 147.

Test yourself

Task 1

Pasaste las vacaciones del año pasado en el hotel Alcázar, en Valencia en España, y decides volver este año. Escribe al director del hotel para hacer una reserva para este verano.

Dale los siguientes detalles:

cuántas personas hay

las habitaciones que quieres

las fechas de tu visita

qué planes tienes para tu visita a Valencia

Dile:

cuándo visitaste su hotel por última vez

por qué te gustó tu estancia allí

Pídele:

más información sobre las excursiones que organiza el hotel.

HOTEL ALCÁZAR
VALENCIA

For talking about future plans you can avoid using the future tense by beginning with Tengo intención de ..., e.g. Tengo intención de aprender a hacer windsurfing.

Note that the introduction to the question begins with the preterite tense:

Pasate las vacaciones del año pasado en el hotel ... = You spent your holiday last year at the hotel....

This is the tense to use for saying when you stayed at the hotel last, i.e. Pasé las vacaciones del año pasado en su hotel.

Suggested phrases for saying why you enjoyed your stay (note that most use the imperfect tense):

Las habitaciones estaban limpias.	= The rooms were clean.
El servicio era atento.	= The service was excellent.
Las vistas son maravillosas.	= The views are magnificent.
La comida era buenísima.	= The food was very good.
La piscina es segura.	= The swimming-pool is safe.

To ask for more information, begin with Le ruego me mande ... (= Please send me ...)

Task 2

Tu familia va a pasar el verano en
Cantabria con unos amigos españoles.
Te mandan información sobre la casa y la región.
Lee la carta y contesta las preguntas poniendo
una (✔) en la casilla correcta.

> León
>
> 10 de mayo 1998
>
> Queridos amigos:
>
> Ya hemos confirmado el apartamento para el verano y os escribo para daros todos los detalles.
>
> Está precisamente a orillas del mar al lado de un bosque. Tiene salón, comedor, cocina y cuatro dormitorios, dos con baño y ducha. También hay un cuarto de baño.
>
> El apartamento está completamente amueblado a buen gusto pero tendremos que llevar nuestras sábanas y toallas.
>
> La limpieza está a la carga de una muchacha que viene diariamente. La he conocido ya y es muy simpática.
>
> Un autobús sale cada quince minutos para el centro de la ciudad y el trayecto dura unos cuarenta minutos. También se puede tomar el tren pero esto sale caro y, además, la estación está bastante lejos.
>
> En las inmediaciones hay facilidades para pescar e ir a caballo.
>
> El alquiler mínimo es de dos meses y por eso mi madre, mi hermana y yo vamos a trasladarnos allí a principios de julio. Papá vendrá más tarde.
>
> Sin más por ahora,
>
> Un abrazo de vuestro amigo
>
> *Juan Carlos*

		No se recomienda	Es posible	No es posible	Es necesario	No es necesario
1	Ir a la costa en coche.					
2	Llevar sábanas y toallas.					
3	Limpiar la casa todos los días.					
4	Ir al centro ciudad en tren.					
5	Preparar la comida.					
6	Ir a la pesca.					
7	Quedarse dos semanas.					
8	Dormir en una habitación con ducha.					

Answers

TASK 2
No se recomienda 4; Es posible 5, 6, 8; No es posible 7;
Es necesario 2; No es necesario 1, 3.

TAKE A BREAK

¡Enhorabuena! You have completed the chapter.

checklist
What you need to know

Can you:

	Fine	Help!
1 say how many weeks' school holiday you have a year and name the holidays?	○	○
2 say where you normally go on holiday?	○	○
3 say who you go with?	○	○
4 say for how long you go?	○	○
5 say what you do on holiday?	○	○
6 ask other people about their holidays?	○	○
7 say how you travel?	○	○
8 describe a recent holiday?	○	○
9 say who you went with?	○	○
10 say for how long you went?	○	○
11 say what the weather was like?	○	○
12 say what you did and what you saw?	○	○
13 give simple opinions about the holiday?	○	○
14 talk about future holiday plans?	○	○
15 ask for details about a town or region you want to visit as a tourist?	○	○

On holiday

You will need to be able to talk about holidays in the past and present tenses. To build up your confidence follow the signposts for helpful hints and check the Mind Maps on pages 115–117. To learn the vocabulary you need to draw your own mind maps and use the Notes/Options in this chapter as models.

Help is at hand!

Notes/Options

1 ¿Cuántas vacaciones escolares tienes?

Durante las Navidades tengo dos semanas de vacaciones.

Navidades = Christmas

... La Pascua ...

La Pascua = Easter

... Semana Santa ...

Semana Santa = Easter break in Spain

Reyes = 6th January: The day of the Three Kings, an official holiday.

Tengo seis semanas durante el verano.

verano = summer

Tengo una semana a mitad del tremestre.

el trimestre = term

... en mayo / primavera.

primavera = spring

... en octubre / otoño.

otoño = autumn

... en invierno.

invierno = winter

2 ¿Dónde vas de vacaciones normalmente?

Normalmente voy a la playa.

Remember! Use the present tense e.g. **Voy**

... a la sierra.

= to the mountains

... al campo.

= to the countryside

No voy a ninguna parte.

= I don't go anywhere.

¿Te alojas en un hotel?

= Do you stay in a hotel?

¿Te quedas en casa de familiares?

= Do you stay with family?

No, me quedo en una pensión.	= I stay in a guest house.
Nos quedamos … Nos alojamos …	= We stay …
Me alojo en un apartamento.	= I stay in an apartment.
Alquilamos una casa.	= We hire a house / cottage.
Hacemos camping.	= We go camping.
Vamos a un albergue juvenil.	= We go to a youth hostel.
¿Te quedas en el Reino Unido o vas al extranjero?	= Do you stay in the U.K. or do you go abroad?
Voy al extranjero. Voy a España / Francia / Grecia / Italia / Turquía.	
Me quedo en Inglaterra / Escocia / Gales / Irlanda.	

3 ¿Con quién vas de vacaciones?   = Who do you go on holiday with?

Voy de vacaciones con mis amigos/as.	= I go on holiday with my friends.
Paso las vacaciones con mi familia.	= I spend my holiday with my family.

4 ¿Por cuánto tiempo estás de vacaciones?

Estoy de vacaciones una semana.	una semana = a week
… quince días.	= … a fortnight

5 ¿Qué haces durante las vacaciones?

Check the Mind Map on
page 115 for more ideas.

Me baño.	= I swim in the sea / river.
Tomo el sol.	= I sunbathe.
Voy de excursión.	= I go on trips.
Meriendo al aire libre.	= I have picnics.
Voy de compras.	= I go shopping.
Visito mi familia.	= I visit my family.

Voy de paseo.	= I go for walks

6 Learn the questions in points 1 to 5 of these Notes/ Options so that you can ask other people about their holidays.

7 ¿Cómo viajas?   = How do you travel?

Voy en barco.	= I go by boat.
… en avión.	= … by plane.
… en tren.	= … by train.
… en ferry.	= … by ferry.
… en coche.	= … by car.
… en autocar.	= … by coach.
… en el AVE.	= … high-speed train (Madrid to Seville).
¿Cuánto tiempo dura el viaje?	= How long is the journey?
Dura siete horas.	= It takes 7 hours.

All these Notes/Options use the present tense. Remember to use time markers such as normalmente and generalmente. Most of the following Notes/Options use the preterite tense.

Check the Mind Maps on page 116
for more help.

8 ¿Dónde fuiste de vacaciones el año pasado?   = Where did you go on holiday last year?

… el verano pasado?	= … last summer
Fui a Irlanda, al campo.	fui = I went
¿Te alojaste en un hotel?	= Did you stay in a hotel?
No, me quedé con mis tíos.	= No, I stayed with my uncle and aunt.
¿Cómo viajaste?	
Fui por coche y ferry.	= I went by car and by ferry.

9 ¿Fuiste con tus amigos?

No, fui con mis padres.	= No, I went with my parents.

47

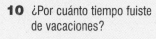

10 ¿Por cuánto tiempo fuiste de vacaciones?

Fui por tres semanas.

11 ¿Qué tiempo hizo durante tus vacaciones? | = What was the weather like during your holiday?

Check the Mind Map on page 117 for weather expressions.

Hizo buen tiempo	= The weather was good.
Hizo mal tiempo.	= The weather was bad.
Hizo sol.	= It was sunny.
Hizo calor.	= It was hot.
Hizo frío.	= It was cold.
Hubo tormentas.	= It was stormy.
Llovió.	= It rained.

12 ¿Qué hiciste durante las vacaciones? | = What did you do during your holidays?

Refer back to point 5 for ideas, but remember to use the preterite tense (see page 147).

Fui a un parque temático.	= I went to a theme park.
Compré recuerdos.	= I bought souvenirs.
Conocí a amigos nuevos.	= I met new friends.
Visité monumentos.	= I visited monuments.

13 ¿Te divertiste? | = Did you have a good time?

¿Lo pasaste bien?	
Me divertí mucho.	
Lo pasé muy bien	
Me encantaron las fiestas.	= I loved the fiestas.
La gente es muy simpática.	= The people are very friendly.
No me gustó la comida.	= I didn't like the food.

Make sure you know Checklist 7 to 12 so that you can ask other people what they did.

14 ¿Vas de vacaciones este verano? | = Are you going on holiday this summer?

¿Dónde vas a ir de vacaciones este verano? | = Where are you going to go on holiday this summer?

¿Qué vas a hacer este verano? | = What are you going to do this summer?

When you are talking about future plans you must either use the future tense (see pages 148–9) or voy a + the infinitive.

15 ¿Qué hay de interés en Córdoba?

¿Hay un museo? | = Is there a museum?

¿Qué hay que hacer en …? | = What is there to do in …?

¿A qué hora cierran las tiendas? | = What time do the shops close?

Look at this model letter asking for details about a town you would like to visit. Learn the highlighted phrases.

2a Beaconsfield Grove
Coventry
Inglaterra
el 3 de abril

Oficina de Turismo
Gerona
España

Muy señor mío:[1]

Voy a pasar quince días[2] en Gerona en el mes de agosto. **Le ruego me envíe**[3] información **sobre la ciudad**[4]. Quisiera un **folleto de datos informativos**[5], **una lista de hoteles**[6] un **plano del centro**[7] y un **mapa de la región**[8].

Le saluda atentamente,

Amina Patel

¹ Dear Sir,

² I am going to spend a fortnight …

³ Please send me …

⁴ … information about the city

⁵ I'd like an information leaflet …

⁶ … a list of hotels

⁷ a plan of the centre

⁸ a map of the region

⁹ Yours faithfully,

See the Mind Map on page 116 to plan answers to the questions in Notes/Options 14 and 15.

Going for a C?

Remember! Examiners will be expecting you to use the present tense to describe what you usually do. They will expect you to use the preterite tense to describe what you did in the past. And they will want you to use the future tense when you talk about what you will do. The holiday topic is one of the best one to show off how well you can use different tenses.

If you have difficulty in remembering your tenses, remember just a few key verbs, such as:

voy = I go

fui = I went

iré = I will go

Test yourself

Task 1

Try this listening exercise. (Side 1, Chapter 5, Foundation). Play the cassette twice.

¿Qué sitio recomienda la empleada?

Task 2

Use this cue card and try to talk for at least two minutes on Mis vacaciones.

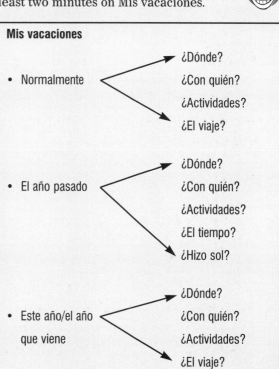

Mis vacaciones

- Normalmente
  - ¿Dónde?
  - ¿Con quién?
  - ¿Actividades?
  - ¿El viaje?

- El año pasado
  - ¿Dónde?
  - ¿Con quién?
  - ¿Actividades?
  - ¿El tiempo?
  - ¿Hizo sol?

- Este año/el año que viene
  - ¿Dónde?
  - ¿Con quién?
  - ¿Actividades?
  - ¿El viaje?

5

Task 3

Lee la carta de Josefina y escribe
una respuesta (100 palabras).

Bilbao, el 10 de septiembre

Querida amiga:

Ya se acabó el verano. ¿Qué tal pasaste las
vacaciones?(1) ¿Te quedaste en casa o fuiste a
algún sitio?(2) ¿Qué hiciste?(3) ¿Hizo buen
tiempo?(4)

Te invito a pasar las Navidades aquí en Bilbao en
mi casa.(5) Puedes venir en el ferry. ¿Cuándo
podrías venir?(6) ¿Qué te gustaría hacer durante
tu visita?(7)

Escríbeme pronto con tu respuesta.

Un saludo,

Josefina

Questions 1 to 4 should be answered in the
preterite tense (see Checklist 8 – 13). You can use
the conditional tense to reply to the invitation to
stay and to say what you would like to do there:
Me gustaría … (see page 149). Don't forget to
thank Josefina for her invitation.

Task 4

Escribe una carta a la oficina de turismo
de Segovia. Pide estas cosas.

1.

2.

3.

4.

Here is some more useful vocabulary for asking
for information about a place. Adapt and add
some of these phrases to your letter to the tourist
office.

un folleto	sobre	la ciudad
		la región
un plano		el camping
un mapa	de	trenes
un horario		autobuses
una lista		restaurantes
		apartamentos para alquilar

TAKE A BREAK

Answers

Task 1

D

5 Mis vacaciones

On holiday

For this topic at this level you need to be able to provide information about places and events. Make sure you can ask questions. Be prepared to give opinions and reasons for your opinions. Using the Notes/Options and the Mind Maps on pages 115–117 to draw your own Mind Map adding opinions for as many of the sections as you can.

Help is at hand!

Notes/Options

1 *Only once you are really sure you are confident with the Foundation Checklist should you carry on with these Higher Notes/Options.*

2 ¿Hay excursiones? = Are there organised trips?

Hay excursiones dos veces a la semana. = There are trips twice a week.

¿Qué días sale la excursión? = What days does the excursion run?

Sale los lunes y los miércoles.

¿Cuándo sale el autocar? = When does the coach leave?

Sale por la mañana.

¿A qué hora es la salida? La hora de la salida es a las ocho. = Departure time is 8 am.

¿A qué hora llegamos? = What time do we arrive?

Llegamos a las 10h. = We arrive at 10am.

¿Dónde es la recogda? = Where is the pick up point?

El autocar le recoge en su hotel. = The coach picks you up at your hotel.

¿Hay plazas libres? = Are there seats available?

Sí, hay plazas libres. = Yes, there are spaces.

No, está completo. = It is fully booked.

checklist
What you need to know

Can you:

	Fine	Help!
1 answer the questions on the Foundation Checklist on page 46?		

If you have ticked any of the Help! boxes, go back to the Foundation Notes/Options to revise!

2 ask for and give information about excursions: location, cost, time?		
3 discuss preferences and opinions about excursions and places of interest?		
4 express preferences for different types of holiday?		

¿Cuánto es?
Son 5.000 pts por persona. | = It is 5,000 pts per person.

¿Está incluida la comida? | = Is lunch included?
Están incluidos el desayuno y la comida. | = Breakfast and lunch are included.

¿Está incluida la entrada? | = Is the entrance fee included?

¿Para en algún pueblo típico? | = Does it stop in any typical village?

Para en La Hoya por media hora. | = It stops in La Hoya for half an hour.

¿A qué distancia está la Granja? | = How far away is La Granja?

¿A cuántos kilómetros está? | = How many kilometres away is it?

Está a unos cien kilómetros. | = It's at about 100 kilometres.

¿Cuál es el itinerario? | = What is the itinerary?

3 ¿Cuál prefieres? ¿Esta o ésa? | = Which do you prefer, this one or that one?

And these?

el mejor / peor museo	= the best / worst museum
la mejor / peor vista panorámica	= the best / worst view
los mejores / peores castillos	= the best / worst castles
las mejores / peores playas	= the best / worst beaches

¿Dónde prefieres ir? ¿Al espectáculo de baile o a visitar las ruinas romanas? | = Where do you prefer to go, to the dance show or to visit the Roman ruins?

A ninguno. No me interesan ni el uno ni el otro. | = Neither. I'm not interested in either.

Prefiero ir de excursión al campo porque hace buen tiempo. | = I prefer to go on a trip to the country because the weather is good.

No quiero ir al castillo porque no me interesa la historia. | = I don't want to go to the castle because I'm not interested in history.

Jamás iré a una corrida de toros. Es demasiado cruel. | = I will never go to a bull fight. It is too cruel.

Do you remember these?

This	**That**
Este castillo	Ese parque temático
Esta excursión	Esa zona
These	**Those**
Estos folletos	Esos paseos
Estas actividades	Esas tiendas

3 En mi opinión …

La mejor excursión es ésta porque hay más que ver. | = In my opinion, this is the best trip because there is more to see.

… el paisaje es más bonito. | = … the scenery is prettier.

… pasa por la costa. | = … it goes along the coast.

Do you remember these?

ninguno/a (os)/(as)	= none / neither
Ninguno de los dos es interesante.	= Neither of the two is interesting.
ni … ni	= either … or
No quiero ir ni al parque temático ni al parque de atracciones.	= I don't want to go to either the theme park or the fun-fair.
nunca	= never
Nunca he viajado en avión.	= I have never travelled by plane.
jamás	= never ever
Jamás he visto cosa tan divertida.	= I have never ever seen such a funny thing.
nunca jamás	= never again
Nunca jamás pediré pulpo.	= I'll never order squid again.

4 ¿Qué tipo de vacaciones prefieres?

Prefiero ir al extranjero, a España por ejemplo.	= I prefer to go abroad, to Spain for example.
Prefiero pasar las vacaciones en el campo	= I prefer to spend my holidays in the country
… porque me gusta descansar.	= … because I like to relax.
Es aburrido y no hay nada que hacer.	= It's boring and there's nothing to do.
Es divertido y hay mucho que hacer.	= It's fun and there's lots to do.
Es un sitio muy tranquilo.	= It is a very quiet place.
… ruidoso.	= … noisy.
… histórico.	
… típico.	
Vale la pena visitar la Costa del Sol.	= It is worthwhile visiting La Costa del Sol.
No vale la pena …	= It is not worth …
Cuando estoy de vacaciones me gusta practicar deporte.	= I like to do sports when I'm on holiday.
Me encanta ir a esquiar.	= I love going skiing.
Durante las vacaciones de invierno voy a esquiar a la sierra.	= During the winter holiday …

Haz Turismo Rural en Castilla y León.

Este fin de semana descubre el Turismo Rural en Castilla y León. Alójate en una habitación con vistas a lo auténtico. Podrás elegir un palacete, molino, monasterio, castillo o entre más de 100 entrañables casas rurales, posadas y centros de Turismo Rural que te esperan con sus puertas abiertas. Disfruta del Turismo Rural, hasta el precio tiene encanto. Y además, hemos creado una infraestructura de centros con la mayor oferta de actividades para todos los gustos: senderismo, aulas de naturaleza, bicicleta de montaña, y excursiones guiadas a parques y espacios naturales de gran interés ecológico. Practica el turismo más auténtico. Vive el encanto de los pueblos, villas y aldeas con la máxima comodidad.

Ven a Castilla y León.
¡Y lo tendrás todo!

Junta de Castilla y León

Say that you'd like to visit the place and say why. You need to use the perfect tense to say that you have not been there (see page 147). Expect a reply that will require you to say why you don't want a beach holiday.

To talk about a holiday you had in the past, use the preterite tense (see page 147).

Test yourself

Task 1

You are going on holiday with your Spanish friend. You see this advert.

You would like to visit Castilla y León. You need to find out if your friend would like to go there. You need to say that you have never been there and that you would like to visit the Spanish countryside. You don't want a beach holiday because you had one at Easter.

You begin the conversation.

You should start the conversation by asking your friend if he / she would like to go to Castilla y León. Expect an answer that will require you to justify your choice. You may be asked a question.

Going for an A?

Listen to the description of a holiday in Castilla y León.

Note down as much information about it as you can. Use the description to write a letter saying why you would like to visit Castilla y León and what you do if you went there. You can use the advert in Task 1 to help you.

podría	= I would be able to
Podría alojarme en un castillo.	
si pudiera	= if I could
Si pudiera ir, visitaría un parque natural.	
si fuera	= if I went
Si fuera, alquilaría una bicileta de montaña.	

Check that you can use the subjunctive (see page 148).

Mi pueblo

checklist
What you need to know

Can you:

		Fine	Help!
1	describe your home town and local area?		
2	say what there is to do there, including festivals?		
3	give simple information and opinions about where you live?		
4	ask where a place is?		
5	say how to get to a place?		
6	understand directions given to you?		
7	give and understand information about using public transport?		
8	understand simple transport signs and notices?		
9	buy tickets for use on public transport?		
10	buy fuel for a car and ask the cost?		
11	ask for the tyres, water and oil to be checked?		
12	understand and describe weather conditions?		

My neighbourhood

This topic can be fun to learn because it's about your town, city, village or area. It is easy to prepare using the Mind Maps (pages 118 and 119) and model answers.

Help is at hand!

Notes/Options

1 tu pueblo. = your town / village
… ciudad. = city
… barrio. = neighbourhood

Es industrial y ruidoso/a. ruidoso/a = noisy

Es grande y moderno/a.

Es pequeño/a y tranquilo/a.

Es histórico/a y turístico/a.

Do you remember these?

Pueblo and barrio are masculine, while ciudad is feminine:

Vivo en una ciudad ruidosa.

but

Mi barrio es muy ruidoso.

¿Dónde está tu barrio?	= Where is your area?
Está al norte / sur / este / oeste de Inglaterra.	= It's in the north / south / east / west of England.
Está en el noroeste.	noroeste = north east
Está a cien kilómetros de Swansea.	= It's a 100 miles from Swansea.
Está en el campo.	= It's in the country.
Está en la costa.	= It's on the coast.
Tiene veinte mil habitantes.	= It has a population of 20,000.

2 ¿Qué hay de interés en tu ciudad para jóvenes?

… para turistas?

= What is there for young people in your city?

= for tourists

una piscina
un estadio
pistas de tenis
un campo de fútbol
grandes almacenes
muchas tiendas
centros comerciales
un mercado
un parque zoológico
un museo
un castillo
una catedral
un teatro

¿Qué se puede hacer en tu pueblo?

= What can you do in your town?

se puede { ir de compras
hacer deporte
ir de excursión

Be prepared to talk about festivals and carnivals in your town.

Hay un carnaval en verano.

= There is a carnival in the summer.

Hay teatro callejero.

= There is street entertainment.

Hay concursos.

= There are competitions.

3 ¿Qué piensas de tu pueblo / ciudad?

= What do you think about your town?

Me gusta porque	hay mucho que hacer. es muy animado/a. tiene buen ambiente. aquí viven mis amigos.
No me gusta porque	no hay nada que hacer. es muy aburrido/a. está contaminado/a. es feo/a y sucio/a.

4 Perdone, señor.

¿Dónde está el ayuntamiento, por favor?

= Excuse me.

= Where is the town hall, please?

5 ¿Por dónde se va a la oficina de turismo?

¿Hay una farmacia por aquí?

= How do you get to the tourist office?

= Is there a chemist around here?

5/6

Have a look at the Mind Map on page 118 about finding places in and around a town.

Suba la calle.

= Go up the street.

Baje la calle.

= Go down the street.

Cruce el puente.

= Cross the bridge.

Siga todo recto / derecho.

= Go straight on.

Tuerza a la derecha.

= Turn right.

Tuerza a la izquierda.

= Turn left.

Tome la primera / segunda / tercera a la izquierda.

= Take the first / second / third on the left.

¿Está lejos?

= Is it far?

¿Está cerca?

= Is it close?

Está después de los semáforos.

= It's after the traffic lights.

La parada está allí.

= The bus-stop is over there.

Dobla la esquina.

= Go round the corner.

Está al final de la calle.

= It's at the end of the street.

Está fuera de la ciudad.

= It's outside the city.

Está en el centro del pueblo.

= It's in the centre of the town.

6

7 Por tren, autocar, autobús y metro

Coja el autobús.	= Take the bus.
Tome el metro.	= Take the underground.
¿A qué hora sale el próximo tren para Madrid?	= What time is the next train to Madrid ?
¿Hay un autocar para Ciudad Real?	= Is there a coach for Ciudad Real?
¿A qué hora llega?	= What time does it arrive?
¿Cuánto tiempo dura el viaje?	= How long is the journey?
Dura / tarda tres horas.	
Es directo o hay que cambiar?	= Is it direct or do you have to change?
Es la próxima parada.	= It's the next stop.
¿Qué línea cojo?	= What line do I take?
¿Dónde está la parada de autobús?	= Where is the bus-stop?
… la estación de ferrocarril / metro?	= … the train / tube station?

8

There's a useful Mind Map on pages 111 and 119 of signs that you will need to recognise.

9 En el despacho de billetes

Quisiera un billete para Salamanca para el día 19, con reserva de asiento.	= I'd like a ticket to Salamanca for the 19th, with a reserved seat.
¿Primera o segunda clase? En segunda.	
¿Ida y vuelta? No, sencillo.	= Return? = No, one way.
¿Cuánto vale? 3000 pts.	
¿Fumador o no fumador? No fumador.	= Smoking or non-smoking?
Quisiera sentarme cerca de la ventanilla, si puede ser.	= I'd like to sit by the window, if possible.
Tome usted. Coche número 12, asiento 72, cerca de la ventanilla.	= Here you are. Carriage no. 12, seat 72, by the window.
Quisiera un bonobús, por favor.	= I'd like a book of 10 bus tickets, please.
¿De qué andén sale el tren a Oviedo?	= Which platform does the Oviedo train leave from?
¿Es éste el andén número dos?	= Is this platform 2?
¿Dónde está la vía 3?	= Where is track 3?

10 En la estación de servicio.

¿Gasolina o gasoil?	= Petrol or diesel?
Llénelo de súper, por favor.	= Fill it up with four-star, please.
¿Me da 25 litros de súper sin plomo?	= Can you give me 25 litres of lead-free four-star?
Póngame 30 litros de gasoil.	= Put in 30 litres of diesel.

11 ¿Algo más?

¿Puede comprobar el aciete?	= Can you check the oil?
Compruebe los neumáticos, por favor.	= Check the tyres, please.
Mire el agua, por favor.	= Check the water, please.

¿Tiene un plano de carreteras?	= Do you have a road map?
¿Hay servicios aquí?	= Are there toilets here?
¿Vende refrescos?	= Do you sell drinks?
¿Es ésta la carretera de Burgos?	= Is this the right road to Burgos?
el autopista	= the motorway

12 El tiempo

Use the Mind Map on page 117 for phrases about the weather.

Going for a C?

Learn the extra vocabulary below to help you understand weather forecasts.

el pronóstico la previsión	= forecast
nieblas / brumas matinales	= morning mist
vientos flojos	= breezes
vientos de componente este	= easterly winds
sin cambio en temperaturas	= no change in temperature
cielo cubierto	= cloudy
cielo claro	= clear sky
aumento de nubosidad	= increase in cloud cover
cielos con intervalos nubosos	= sunny intervals
alguna llovizna	= some showers
un empeoramiento	= worsening
un mejoramiento	= an improvement
inestable	= unstable

Test yourself

Task 1

Listen to the cassette (Side 1, Chapter 6, Foundation). Play the cassette twice. Listen to the following station announcements.

Pon una marca en las casillas correctas.

1 El tren sale a las
   a   3h 30
   b   13h 30
   c   13h 20

2 El tren llega al andén número
   a   5
   b   15
   c   25

3 El tren tren llega a las
   a   2h 40
   b   12h 14
   c   20h 4

4 El tren sale de la vía
   a   7
   b   17
   c   6

Task 2

You are in a service-station in Spain. Your teacher will play the part of the attendant and will start the conversation.

1 Buenos días, ¿Qué desea?

2 Muy bien.

3 En seguida, señor(ita).

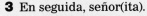

4 Hay que seguir todo recto.

20km?
30km?
60km?
45km?

5 Está a 50 kilómetros de aquí.

Sí están allí, a la derecha de la caja.

¡Ojo! (Watch out!) You may be marked down if you use the 'tú' form of the verbs rather than the 'Usted'.

Task 3

Empareja los dibujos con las frases.

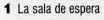

1 La sala de espera

a

2 La consigna

b

3 El cambio de moneda

c

4 Caballeros

d

Task 4

Escribe una carta a tu corresponsal español/a. Describe tu pueblo. (80 palabras)

Use this formula to help you.

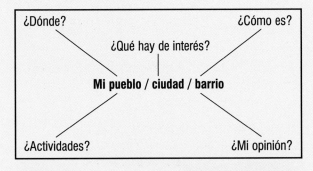

¿Dónde?   ¿Cómo es?

¿Qué hay de interés?

Mi pueblo / ciudad / barrio

¿Actividades?   ¿Mi opinión?

TAKE A BREAK

Remember to look back at the Checklist!

6

My neighbourhood

At Higher you must be about to talk about your country and compare it with a Spanish-speaking country as well as to be able to talk about your local. Make sure you know something about the geography, weather, industries, education system, food, customs and festivals of Spain.

Have a brain-storming session and jot down some facts you have picked up in the time you have been learning Spanish.

Using the notes below prepare a short presentation about those aspects so that you won't be surprised if you are required to talk or write about Spanish life.

Help is at hand!

Notes/Options

1 *Only once you are really sure you are confident with the Foundation Checklist should you carry on with these Higher Notes/Options.*

2 más … que … = more … than …
menos … que … = less … than …
mejor que … = better than …
peor que … = worse than …

El clima es más frío aquí.

El clima es menos caluroso.

caluroso = hot
húmedo = humid
seco = dry

Hacer mejor / peor tiempo. = The weather is better / worse.

Llueve más …
Nieva menos …
Hace más viento.
Hay menos tormentas.
Hace más sol.
El paisaje es más verde.
La región es menos agrícola.
El campo es más montañoso.
La cuidad es menos tranquila.

Mi pueblo

checklist
What you need to know

Can you:

		Fine	Help!
1	answer the questions on the Foundation Checklist on page 54?		

If you have ticked the Help! box, go back to the Foundation Notes/Options to revise.

		Fine	Help!
2	understand and make comparisons between your country and a Spanish-speaking country?		
3	express and explain opinions about where you live?		
4	describe local festivals?		
5	explain preferences about travel?		
6	give details about a vehicle breakdown?		
7	report an accident?		

3 ¿Cuáles son las ventajas y desventajas de tu pueblo?

animado/a	= lively
peligroso/a	= dangerous

No me gusta mi pueblo / ciudad / barrio / región porque …

hace buen tiempo

hay mucho que hacer para jóvenes

es antiguo/a e histórico/a

está cerca de la playa / costa / sierra / montaña

está en la costa / sierra / montaña

el clima es malo

está lejos del centro / la capital

viven lejos mis amigos/as

no hay nada que hacer para la gente jóven

es muy sucio y ruidoso

hay contaminación y mucho tráfico

basura	= rubbish
bosques	= forests
lagos	= lakes
que hacer	= to do

4 Las fiestas

If you get a question on fiestas bear in mind their social importance in Spain. Every village, town and city in Spain has a local festival to celebrate their patron saint. For example Pamplona celebrates San Fermín with the running of the bulls. Bull fighting is a feature of most fiestas but there are plenty of other activities. Most of the fiestas have a religious origin, such as Carnival, but some, like the Feria de Sevilla, are founded in folklore. Fiestas can last up to a week and involve the whole community.

Semana Santa — = Holy Week *(the week leading up to Easter – this is when Spaniards have their Easter holidays)*

En Sevilla la Semana Santa se celebra con procesiones religiosas espectaculares.

Viernes Santo — = Good Friday

Se llevan imágenes de Jesús y María por las calles.

Nochebuena — = Christmas Eve (this is celebrated more than Christmas Day in Spain)

En Nochebuena vamos a la Misa del Gallo. — Misa de Gallo = Midnight Mass

Toda la familia se reune para cenar juntos. — = All the family get together to have dinner.

El Día de Navidad — = Christmas Day

En casa tenemos un belén. — = At home we have a Nativity scene.

También se mandan tarjetas. — = Cards are also sent.

Hay gente que tiene un árbol de Navidad. — = Some people have Christmas trees.

Noche Vieja — = New Year's Eve

En Madrid la gente se reune en la plaza de la Puerta del Sol. — se reune = gathers

Para tener buena suerte en el Año Nuevo tienes que comerte 12 uvas antes de que termine de tocar las doce el reloj de la Puerta del Sol. — = For good luck in the New Year you have to eat 12 grapes before the Puerta del Sol clock strikes 12.

La Puerta del Sol — (= clock in the main square in Madrid.)

Hay bailes y música.

Hay fuegos artificiales. — = There are fireworks.

El Día de Reyes — 6th January (The Day of the Three Kings)

En Reyes los niños reciben regalos.

En cada ciudad hay un desfile de Reyes. — desfile = parade

Tres personas famosas se disfrazan de los Reyes. — = Three personalities dress up as the Wise Men.

Distribuyen jugetes a los niños de la ciudad. — = They give out presents to the city children.

La gente se divierte. — = People enjoy themselves.

5 ¿Cómo prefieres viajar?

Check the Mind Map on page 116 for more transport vocabulary.

Prefiero viajar en avión porque es rápido.

Prefiero viajar en bici porque es ecológico.

Prefiero viajar a pie porque es saludable.

6

Mi coche tiene una avería.	= My car has broken down.
El neumático tiene un pinchazo.	= The tyre has a puncture.
Tengo el parabrisas roto.	= I've got a smashed windscreen.
¿Qué marca de coche es?	= What make is the car?

7

Ha habido un accidente.	= There has been an accident.
El conductor está herido.	= The driver is hurt.
Los pasajeros …	= The passengers …
Hay que llamar a un ambulancia.	= We need to call an ambulance.
El coche chocó con un camión.	= The car hit a lorry.
La moto iba con demasiada velocidad.	= The motorbike was going too fast.
Tomé nota de la matrícula.	= I took the registration number.
Era la culpa del conductor.	= It was the driver's fault.
No había testigos.	= There were no witnesses.

Going for an A?

Make sure you know you the preterite form of radical changing and irregular verbs. See page 149.

Test yourself

Task 1

Listen to the cassette (Side 1, Chapter 6, Higher). Play the cassette twice.

Answer the following questions **in English**.

1 What does the student not like about British weather? (1 mark)

2 According to the student, to what extent are the British and Spanish aware of each other's traditional festivals? Give full details. (3 marks)

Task 2

Durante unas vacaciones en España con tu familia tenéis un accidente de coche. Escribe un informe para la compañía de seguros. (120 palabras) En tu informe contesta las siguientes preguntas:

¿Dónde y cómo ocurrió?

¿Qué vehículos fueron afectados por el accidente?

¿Qué daños sufrió tu coche?

¿Resultaron heridos?

¿Qué hiciste después del accidente?

Task 1

1 It is changeable.

2 The English think the Spanish have fiestas every day, while the Spanish have never heard of English festivals. There are not so many festivals in England as in Spain. The student thinks that those festivals he has seen are very interesting.

Task 2 (Suggested Answer)

El accidente ocurrió en la esquina de la calle del Milaro y la Carretera de Burgos. Un camión francés circulando a una velocidad de 30 kilómetros por hora, salió de la Calle del Milagro y chocó contra nuestro coche que iba a 50 kilómetros por hora por la carretera. Nuestro coche, un Ford Escort, sufrió daños extensos y está averiado. El parabrisas se rompió y el neumático izquierdo delantero tiene un pinchazo.

Mi madre, que era la pasajera en el asiento delantero estaba herida, se rompió el brazo. El conductor del camión no se paró. Después de ocurrir el accidente llamé a los servicios de emergencia.

De compras

checklist
What you need to know

Can you:

		Fine	Help!
1	ask for certain shops?	○	○
2	ask about opening times?	○	○
3	ask for certain foods?	○	○
4	ask for different quantities?	○	○
5	say that is all you want?	○	○
6	pay, and check the change?	○	○
7	name items of clothing?	○	○
8	give your own clothes size?	○	○
9	ask for particular colours / materials?	○	○
10	give opinions on clothes?	○	○
11	ask if credit cards are accepted?	○	○
12	ask where a post office / letter box is?	○	○
13	say you want to send a letter?	○	○
14	ask how long it will take?	○	○
15	ask how much it costs?	○	○
16	ask for stamps?	○	○
17	ask if there is a telephone?	○	○
18	ask for a phone card?	○	○
19	give your telephone number?	○	○
20	ask about a reverse charge call?	○	○
21	tell someone how to make a phone call?	○	○

Let's go shopping!

This topic will most likely come up in the Listening and Speaking sections of the exam, although you may be required to write a shopping list or a short description of a shopping trip. There is a lot of vocabulary. Use the Mind Maps on pages 120–121 to help you memorise as much as possible. Make sure you can ask questions as well as answer them.

Help is at hand!

Notes/Options

1 ¿Dónde está la carnicería?	= Where is the butcher's?
… el estanco?	= … the tobacconist's.
… la farmacia / droguería?	= … the chemist?
… la frutería?	= … the greengrocer's?
… la librería?	= … the bookshop?
… la panadería?	= … the bakery?
… la pastelería?	= … the cake shop?
… la pescadería?	= … the fishmonger's?
… la peluquería?	= ... the hairdresser's?
… la tienda de comestibles / la tienda de ultramarinos?	= … grocer's?
… la tienda de discos?	= … music shop?
… la tienda de recuerdos?	= … the souvenir shop?
… la zapatería?	= … the shoe shop?

¡Ojo! (Watch out!) You don't buy medicines at the droguería, that's where you get make-up and toiletries. The farmacia stocks the medicines. An estanco is licensed to sell stamps and tobacco. It also stocks other items such as stationery, postcards and newspapers.

¡Ojo! A librería is a bookshop, not a library. A library is a biblioteca.

2 ¿A qué hora cierra la tienda? = What time does the shop close?

Abierto de 10h a 1h y de 4h a 7h. = Open from 10am to 1pm and from 4 pm to 7 pm.

Cerrado domingos, festivos y vísperas de festivos. = Closed on Sundays, holidays and eves of holidays

Abierto de 9h a 21h sin interrupción. = Open continuously from 9 am to 9 pm.

Cerrado por la tarde. = Closed in the afternoon.

3 ¿Hay …? = Is / Are there any …?

… pan? = … bread?
… aceitunas? = … olives?
… jamón? = … ham?

Look at the Mind Map on page 121 to revise food items.

4

Cantidades			
Quiero/Quisiera un kilo	de	chorizo	= 1k spicy sausage
medio kilo		queso	= $\frac{1}{2}$ k cheese
un cuarto kilo		sardinas	= $\frac{1}{2}$ k sardines
doscientos gramos		melocotones	= 200gm peaches
una lata		aceitunas	= a tin of olives
un cartón		leche	= a carton of milk
un paquete		caramelos	= a packet of sweets
una barra		pan	= a loaf of bread
una tableta		chocolate	= a bar of chocolate
un pedazo		carne	= a piece of meat
una docena		huevos	= a dozen eggs
media docena		panecillos	= half a dozen buns
una botella		aceite	= a bottle of oil
un litro		agua mineral	= 1litre mineral water
medio litro		zumo de naranja	= $\frac{1}{2}$ litre orange juice

¿Deme una docena de huevos? = Can I have a dozen eggs?

¿Póngame un kilo de manzanas? = Can I have a kilo of apples?

¿De qué tamaño? = What size?

Un paquete grande.

El tamaño pequeño.

5 ¿Algo más? = Anything else?

No, nada más. = No, that's all.

Un poco más. = A bit more.

Ya es bastante. / Basta ya. = That's enough.

Está bien. = That's fine.

6 ¿Cuanto es? = How much is it?

¿A cuánto están las zanahorias? = How much are the carrots?

¿Cuánto es el melón? = How much is the melon?

Los plátanos están a 100 pts el kilo. = The bananas are 100 pesetas a kilo.

Las coliflores están a 50 pts cada una. = The cauliflowers are 50 pesetas each.

Sólo tengo un billete de mil. = I've only got a 1000 pesetas note.

Tome el cambio. = Here is the change.

el dinero	= money
el cambio	= change
un billete	= note
una moneda	= coin
un duro	= 5pts piece
No tengo ni un duro.	= I don't have a penny.

Make sure you know your numbers. See page 157.

7

See the Mind Map on page 120 to revise clothes and accessories.

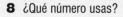

8 ¿Qué número usas? = What (shoe) size are you?

¿Qué talla tienes? = What (clothes) size are you?

Guía de números									
Zapatos									
Reino Unido	2	3	4	5	6	7	8	9	10
España	35	36	37	38	39	40	41	42	43
Tallas									
Reino Unido	6	8	10	12	14	16			
España	34	36	38	40	42	44			

9 ¿De qué color? = What colour?

En rojo no hay. = There are no red ones.

No quedan en rojo. = There are no red ones left.

Sólo hay en amarillo. = There are only yellow ones.

See page 103 to revise colours.

las telas	**= fabrics**	de plástico	= plastic
de algodón	= cotton	de lycra	= lycra
de lana	= wool	**los metales**	**= metals**
de seda	= silk	de oro	= gold
de cuero	= leather	de plata	= silver

¿Tiene una falda de lana en azul? = Do you have a blue, woollen skirt?

Quisiera un par de pendientes de plata. = I'd like a pair of silver earrings.

Quiero un reloj de oro. = I'd like a gold watch.

10 Me gusta **el** vestido. Me **lo** llevo. = I like the dress. I'll take it.

Me gustan **los** zapatos. Me **los** llevo. = I like the shoes. I'll take them.

Me gustan **las** botas. Me **las** llevo. = I like the boots. I'll take them.

No me gusta **la** chaqueta. **La** dejo. = I don't like the jacket. I'll leave it.

Me gusta(n) No me gusta (n)	porque	es	largo/a corto/a elegante grande pequeño/a blanco/a feo/a bonito/a cómodo/a incómodo/a barato/a caro/a
		son	largos/as cortos/as elegantes grandes pequeños/as blancos/as feos/as bonitos/as cómodo/a incómodos/as baratos/as caros/as
		están no están	de moda

demasiado = too	muy = very
Es demasiado largo.	Es muy caro.
Son demasiado cortos.	Son muy baratos.

No me gusta el color.

Prefiero el abrigo verde.

Prefiero el verde.

11 ¿Acepta tarjetas de crédito?

12 ¿Por dónde se va a correos? = How do you get to the post office?

¿Hay un buzón por aquí? = Is there a post box round here?

13 Quisiera mandar una carta a Inglaterra. = I want to send a letter to England.

Quiero mandar unas postales a Gales. = I want to send some postcards to Wales.

Quiero enviar un paquete a Escocia. = I want to send a parcel to Scotland.

14 ¿Cuánto tiempo tarda en llegar? = How long does it take to arrive?

¿Cuántos días tarda en llegar?

= How many days does it take to arrive?

15 ¿Cuánto vale mandar una carta a Alemania?

= How much does it cost to send a letter to Germany?

16 Quiero cuatro sellos de 30 pts.

= I'd like four 30 pesetas stamps.

Quiero un sello para el Reino Unido.

= I'd like a stamp for the U.K.

17 ¿Hay una cabina de teléfono cerca de aquí?

= Is there a phone box near here?

18 Quisiera una tarjeta telefónica.

= I'd like a phone card.

19 ¿Cuál es tu/su número de teléfono?
Mi número de teléfono es el 26 54 82.

20 Quiero hacer una llamada a cobro revertido.

= I'd like to make a reverse charge call.

Test yourself

Task 1

Listen to the cassette (Side 1, Chapter 7, Foundation). Play the cassette twice.

Estás en una tienda de ultramarinos cuando oyes esta conversación entre un cliente y la tendera.

Debes indicar si el clinete compra el artículo (✔) o no (X). También debes indicar la cantidad que compra o la razón por la que no compra.

 No hay _____ ☐ _____

☐ _____   ☐ _____

☐ _____   ☐ _____

Going for a C?

Expand your descriptions with basic opinions and give simple reasons for your views. You could use, for example:

A

Read the instructions for using a Spanish phone box and match the pictures to the phrases. The instructions are not in the correct order.

B

Now put the phrases and pictures in the correct order.

1 Coloque las monedas en la ranura.

2 Espere el tono.

3 Marque el indicativo.

4 Utilize monedas de 10pts, 25pts y 100 pts.

5 Marque el número.

e)

a)   b)

c)    d)

001 842 33 567   0·0·1–...

7

Task 2

You are in a post office in Spain. Your teacher will play the part of the post office clerk and will start the conversation.

Buenos días, ¿qué desea?

¿Para cartas?

Y, ¿para dónde son?

¿Algo más?

Son 110 pesetas.

Ahí, está, al lado de la puerta.

Task 3

A

You are about to enter a shop and you see this sign on the door. What does the sign tell you?

B

You want to buy some meat. Which sign would you follow?

TAKE A BREAK

Remember to look back at the Checklist!

7

De compras

Let's go shopping!

Prepare a talk about your shopping habits: say where you shop, who pays for your clothes, what sort of shops stock what you like and where the shops are. Describe a recent shopping trip and one you are planning. Say what you are going to buy the various members of your family for their birthdays. Use the Notes/Options below and the Mind Maps on pages 120–121 to help you.

Help is at hand!

Notes/Options

1 *Once you've looked back at the Foundation Checklist, and you feel confident, carry on with the Higher level!*

2 En los grandes almacenes

• 4 • Hogar Electrodomésticos Cafetería y Restaurante Regalos	= home and electrical goods = gifts
• 3 • Muebles y Decoración Agencia de viajes Electrónica Sonido Televisión	= furnishings = travel agency = home entertainment systems
• 2 • Moda mujer Zapatería Peluquería de señoras Artículos de cuero	= women's fashions and shoes = women's hairdresser = leather goods
• 1 • Moda jóvenes Deportes Jugetería Moda infantil	= teenage fashions and sports = toys and children's fashions
• B • Moda hombres Perfumería Papelería Librería CDs	= men's fashions = perfumes = stationery = book shop and CDs
• S • Ferretería Supermercado	= hardware = supermarket

checklist
What you need to know

Can you:

	Fine	Help!
1 complete the Foundation Checklist on page 62?		

If you have ticked the Help! box, go back to the Foundation Checklist and revise.

Shopping

2 find your way around a department store?

3 state and explain preferences about clothes and fashion?

4 make a complaint in a shop explaining the problem and asking for a replacement or refund?

5 understand information about discounts, special offers, reductions and sales?

6 discuss general shopping habits?

Lost property

7 report the loss of an item stating what you have lost, where and when?

At the money exchange

8 exchange money or travellers cheques?

9 ask about the rate of exchange?

10 ask for coins and notes of a certain type?

Vamos a la sección de caballeros.	= Let's go to the menswear department.
Está en el sótano.	= It's in the basement.
… la primera planta / el primer piso.	= … the first floor.
Subimos por la escalera mecánica.	= Let's go up the escalator.
… el ascensor.	= … in the lift.
Hay que pagar en la caja.	= You pay at the cash desk.

3 Me encanta la moda deportiva. = I love casual fashions.

la moda callejera.	= street fashions
la moda clásica	= classic fashions
Prefiero llevar vaqueros y una camiseta.	= I prefer to wear jeans and a T-shirt.
Odio el uniforme de mi colegio.	= I hate my school uniform.
Estar a la moda no es muy importante.	= Being fashionable is not very important.
Tengo mi propio estilo.	= I have my own style.
No me gusta vestir como todo el mundo.	= I don't like dressing like everybody else.
La ropa no es importante para mí.	= Clothes are not important to me.
Estoy más cómodo/a en un chandal.	= I'm most comfortable in a track suit.
El aspecto personal es importante.	= Personal appearance is important.

4 Problemas

en general	**= in general**	
No funciona.	= It doesn't work.	
Está roto/a.	= It's broken.	
la ropa	**= clothes**	
Hay una mancha.	= There is a stain.	
Falta un botón.	= There is a button missing.	

Quiero devolver este artículo.	= I want to return this item.
¿Tiene el recibo?	= Do you have the receipt?
Tome el recibo.	= Here is the receipt.
No, no lo tengo porque fue un regalo.	= No, I don't have it because it was a present.
¿Quiere cambiarlo para otra cosa?	= Do you want to change it for something else?
Prefiero un reembolso.	= I prefer a refund.
Quiero cambiarlo para otra cosa.	= I want to change it for something else.

5
rebajas	= sale
descuento	= discount

PROMOCIÓN	**PROMOTION**
OFERTA ESPECIAL	**SPECIAL OFFER**
EN LA SECCIÓN DE JOYERÍA	**IN JEWELLERY DEPARTMENT**
Gran surtido de joyas	**Big selection of jewellery**
Relojes de marca a precios reducidos	Designer watches at reduced prices
Grandes rebajas en pulseras	Big sale of bracelets
Grandes reducciones en precios de collares de oro y plata	Big price reductions on gold and silver necklaces
Gran liquidación de pendientes	Big sale of earrings
Descuentos sorprendentes en cadenas de oro	Amazing discounts on gold chains
Los mejores precios	**The best prices**

Remember! Adjectives (describing words) in Spanish go after the word they are describing. Occasionally they go in front, and this is to add emphasis. Note that **grande** *becomes* **gran** *when in front of the word it is describing. Practise the phrases in the advert above by making up another advert / sales notice about a variety of goods.*

6 ¿Dónde haces las compras?

De vez en cuando hago las compras para mi familia.	= I sometimes do the shopping for my family.
Voy al supermercado todos los sábados.	= I go to the supermarket every Saturday.
Compro todas las cosas en el supermercado.	= I buy everything in the supermarket.
No quiero perder tiempo yendo de tienda en tienda.	= I don't want to waste time going from shop to shop.
Compro la fruta y las verduras / legumbres en el mercado.	= I buy the fruit and vegetables in the market.
Compro el pan en la panadería en la esquina de la calle.	= I buy the bread from the bakery on the corner.
Me encanta ir a ver tiendas con mis amigos/as.	= I love window shopping with my friends.

7 Objetos perdidos — **= Lost property**

He perdido mi bolso. — = I have lost my bag.
… mi cámara.
… mi monedero
… mi billetero
… mi pasaporte.
… mi maleta.

Me han robado.	= I have been robbed.
¡Un ladrón me ha robado la cámara!	= A thief has stolen my camera!
¿Cuándo ocurrió el robo?	= When did the robbery take place?
¿Cuándo lo/la perdió?	= When did you lose it?
Lo/la perdí anoche.	= I lost it last night.
hace una hora	= an hour ago
esta mañana	= this morning
¿Dónde lo/la perdió?	= Where did you lose it?

Lo/la perdí en el autobús.	= I lost it on the bus.
¿De qué marca es?	= What make is it?
¿Qué contiene?	
Contiene mis tarjetas de crédito y 10 mil pts.	
Es de cuero.	= It's leather.

Make sure you know the preterite and perfect forms of *perder*, *dejar* and *robar* – essential for reporting lost property.

8 En el cambio	**= At the exchange counter**
¿Dónde puedo cambiar dinero?	= Where can I change money?
¿Se pueden cambiar cheques de viajero aquí?	= Can I change travellers cheques here?
¿Quiere usted firmar los cheques?	= Will you sign the cheques?
No tengo ningún dinero español.	= I don't have any Spanish money.
9 ¿A cuánto está la libra?	= What is the rate of exchange for sterling?
10 ¿Puede darme unos billetes de doscientas pesetas?	= Can you give me some 200 pesetas snotes?
¿Se pueden cambiar monedas?	
Deme unas monedas de cien pesetas, por favor.	= Give me some 100 pesetas coins, please.
Nunca cambiamos monedas.	= We don't change coins.
¿Hay que pagar comisión?	= Is there a commission?
Sí, hay 200 pesetas de comisión.	= There is a 200 pesetas commission.

Test yourself

Task 1

Listen to the girl talking about her shopping habits (Side 1, Chapter 7, Higher). Listen twice to this piece on the cassette.

¿Qué diferencias hay entre Carmen y tú?

Task 2

You are in a Spanish city and your suitcase is stolen. You go to the police station. Your teacher will ask you the following questions in the part of the policeman / woman.

Buenos días. ¿Qué te pasa?

1 Explica que te han robado la maleta y cuándo ocurrió.

¿Dónde estabas y qué hacías?

2 Dile dónde estabas y qué hacías cuando ocurrió el robo.

Y, ¿sabes quién la tomó?

3 Haz una descripción del ladrón.

¿Cómo es la maleta y qué contiene?

4 Contesta a la pregunta del / de la policía.

Vale. ¿Dónde estás alojado/a?

5 Explica dónde estás alojado/a y hasta cuándo.

Bueno, vamos a ver si la encontramos.

Task 3

You are shopping in Spain. Your parents don't speak any Spanish and they ask you to help them.

Why would it be a good idea to do your shopping in Galerías Preciados?

> **Ahora tienes más motivos que nunca para seguir con Galerías.**
>
> **Porque te ofrecemos la gran oportunidad de comprarte lo que estabas deseando, con un descuento realmente sorprendente.**
>
> ## GALERIAS PRECIADOS

Task 4

Cuando regresas a Inglaterra, tu padre tiene problemas con el reloj nuevo que compró en los grandes almacenes en Burgos. Escribe una carta al director con los siguientes detalles:

- fecha de compra
- garantía
- problema
- precio
- recibo
- cómo y cuándo quieres que el director resuelva el problema. (100-120 palabras)

Remember to keep it formal. See Chapter 5, pages 48–49, for some useful letter writing expressions.

Answers

TASK 1

Use the Notes/Options in this chapter and make up your answer.

TASK 2

Suggested answers for roleplay.

1 Me han robado la maleta. Ocurrió esta mañana.

2 Estaba en la estación de autobuses. Dejé la maleta al lado de un asiento cuando fui a comprar un billete.

3 El ladrón es alto, moreno, con el pelo rizado. Llevaba una chaqueta gris.

4 La maleta es nueva. Es de plástico azul. Contiene ropa y libros.

5 Estoy alojado en el hotel Canovas hasta el 6 de septiembre

TASK 3

Discount.

TASK 4

Suggested Answer

Estimado señor:

Me dirijo a usted para hacer una reclamación con respeto a un reloj que compró mi padre en sus almacenes el mes de agosto. El reloj no funciona. Es un Omega de oro. Costó 10.000 pesetas. Está bajo garantía hasta el 20 de agosto del próximo.

Mando adjunto el reloj y el recibo. Le ruego me cambie el reloj por otro de la misma marca lo antes posible.

Le saluda atentamente.

8 En el restaurante

Eating out

This topic will probably come up in the Listening and Speaking sections of the exam. To familiarise yourself with the vocabulary, you could record the model answers below on to a blank cassette and listen to it at odd moments of the day.

Help is at hand!

Notes/Options

1 ¿Te gusta el pollo? = Do you like chicken?

Sí, me gusta el pollo. = I like chicken.
  me gusta mucho. = I like it very much.
  me encanta = I love it.

¿Cuál es tu plato preferido? = What is your favourite dish?

Mi plato preferido es espagueti con salsa. = My favourite dish is spaghetti with sauce.

Está bueno/a. = It is good.
Estaba bueno/a. = It was good.
… buenísimo/a. = … really good
… delicioso/a. = … delicious
… rico/a. = … tasty
… riquísimo/a. = … very tasty

No como carne. = I don't eat meat.

No me gusta la carne. = I don't like meat.

No me gusta nada. = I don't like it at all.

Odio la carne. = I hate meat.

Me da asco. = It makes me sick.

checklist
What you need to know

Can you:

		Fine	Help!
1	express simple opinions about food?	●	●
2	ask for a table for yourself / a group?	●	●
3	reserve a table?	●	●
4	accept / refuse offers of food and drink?	●	●
5	attract the waiter / waitress's attention?	●	●
6	ask for food and items on the table?	●	●
7	ask about availability / recommendations of food and drink?	●	●
8	ask for the menu?	●	●
9	ask for a set meal?	●	●
10	choose and order drinks, snacks and meals?	●	●
11	ask for an explanation of something on the menu?	●	●
12	ask for things missing from the table?	●	●
13	complain about a meal?	●	●
14	express opinions about a meal?	●	●
15	ask for and settle the bill?	●	●

2 Quisiera una mesa para cuatro personas, por favor. = I'd like a table for four, please.

3 Quisiera reservar una mesa para mí y mi familia. = I'd like a table for myself and my family.

¿Ha reservado una mesa? = Have you reserved a table?

Sí, he reservado una mesa.

Reservé una mesa esta mañana por teléfono. = I reserved a table this morning by phone.

4 ¿Quieres ensalada? = Do you want salad?

Quiere … *This is the polite form.*

¿Quieres más postre? = Do you want more dessert?

Sí, quiero ensalada. = Yes, I'd like salad.
… más = … more

¿Te sirvo sopa? = Shall I serve you some soup?

¿Le sirvo …? *This is the polite form.*

¿Tienes sed? = Are you thirsty?

He comido bastante. = I have eaten enough.

Estoy lleno/a. = I'm full.

5 ¡Oiga, camarero! = Waiter!
… camarera! = Waitress!

6 Pásame la sal. = Pass me the salt.

Páseme … *This is the polite form.*

¿Me puedes pasar la pimienta? = Can you pass me the pepper?

¿Me puede …? *This is the polite form.*

7 ¿Hay calamares? = Is there any squid?

¿Qué legumbres hay? = What vegetables are there?

¿Qué recomienda usted? = What do you recommend?

Recomiendo el bacalao. = I recommend the cod.

¿Qué tiene/hay de postre? = What do you have for dessert?

8 ¿Me puede traer la carta, por favor? = Can you bring me the menu, please?

9 Quiero el menú de 5000 pts. = I'd like the 5000 pesetas set meal.

… el plato combinado = *(A quick cheap meal consisting of a selection of food all together on one plate.)*

Sí gracias, tengo hambre. = Yes please, I'm hungry.

… sed. = … thirsty.

No gracias, no tengo hambre. = No thank you, I'm not hungry.

¿Tienes hambre? = Are you hungry?

¿Tiene …? *This is the polite form.*

10 ¿Qué vas a tomar? = What are you going to have?

¿Qué va …? *This is the polite form.*

Quiero pedir, por favor. = I'd like to order, please.

¿Podemos pedir? = Can we order?

Para mi / él / ella / ellos(as) / nosotros … = For me / him / her / them / us …

Quiero … = I want …

Quisiera … = I'd like …

De primero … = For first course …

De primer plato …

Para empezar … = For starters …

De segundo …

De segundo plato …

Después … = Followed by …

De postre … = For dessert …

¿Y para beber? = And (what would you like) to drink?

una botella de vino tinto de la casa = a bottle of house red

una copa de vino blanco = a glass of white wine

agua mineral con gas = sparkling mineral water

… sin gas = still mineral water

una jarra de sangría = a jug of sangría

una fanta

Take a look at the Mind Maps on page 122 to see if you know the words for drinks, snacks and dishes.

11 ¿Qué es gazpacho? = What is gazpacho?

Es una sopa de tomates, pepinos y cebolla. = It is a soup made of tomatoes, cucumbers and peppers.

Se sirve frío. = It is served cold.

¿En qué consiste una paella? = What does a paella consist of?

Es un plato de mariscos y legumbres cocido con arroz. = It is a seafood and vegetable dish cooked with rice.

¿Qué es una tortilla española?

Es una fritura de huevos y patatas. = It's eggs and potatoes fried together.

¿Qué son las tapas?

Son raciones pequeñas de comida que se sirven en platillos. = They are snacks served on small dishes.

¿Qué es la sangría?

Es una bebida hecha con vino tinto, limonada, un poquito de coñac y fruta cortada que se sirve fría en una jarra. = It is a drink made with red wine, lemonade, a little bit of brandy and pieces of fruit, served chilled in a jug.

Es muy refrescante. = It is very refreshing.

12 ¡Oiga, camare~~ro~~, tenedor. = Waiter! There is a fork missing.
… un cuchillo. = … a knife …
… una cuchara. = … a spoon …
… un plato. = … a plate …
… una copa. = … a glass (for wine and liqueurs).
… un vaso. = … a glass (for water / soft drinks).
… una taza. = … a cup …
… una servilleta. = … a napkin …

No hay aceite y vinagre. = There is no oil and vinegar.

13 El mantel está sucio. = The table cloth is dirty.

Tengo una copa sucia. = I have got a dirty glass.

La comida está fría. = The food is cold.

Pedí una chuleta muy hecha. = I asked for a well cooked chop.
… poca hecha. = … rare …

14 ¡Qué aproveche! = Enjoy your meal!

¿Le gustó la comida? = Did you enjoy your meal?

¿Has comido bien? = Have you eaten well?

¿Ha …? *This is the polite form.*

He comido muy bien. = I have eaten very well.

Also look back to Notes/Options 1.

15 La cuenta, por favor. = The bill, please.

Queremos pagar la cuenta. = We'd like to settle the bill.

¿Están incluidas las bebidas? = Are the drinks included?

¿Está incluido el servicio? = Is service included?
… el IVA? = … VAT?

¿Acepta tarjetas de crédito? = Do you accept credit cards?

Hay un error en la cuenta. = There is a mistake on the bill.

No tomamos patatas fritas. = We didn't have chips.

Hay que dejar propina. = You have to leave a tip.

¿Qué dejamos de propina? = What shall we leave as a tip?

Going for a C?

Remember that talking about food can come up in other topics such as holidays. Be ready to talk about the kinds of food you eat abroad.

Me encanta la comida española. = I love Spanish food.

Comí de todo. = I ate all sorts of things.

Probé los calamares. = I tried squid.

Me gustó / gustaron mucho. = I liked it / them a lot.

Me daba/n asco. = It / They made me feel sick.

Era/n demasiado salado/a/s. = It / They were too salty.
… picante/s. = … hot / spicy.
… dulce/s. = … sweet.

No tenía/n sabor. = It / They had no flavour.

Test yourself

Task 1

Listen to the cassette (Side 1, Chapter 8, Foundation). Play the cassette twice.

1 Entras en el restaurante. El camarero quiere saber algo. ¿Qué quiere saber?

2 ¿Dónde está la mesa?

3 ¿Qué va a traer el camarero?

4 ¿Qué recomienda el camarero?

5 Una amiga habla con el camarero. ¿Qué hay en la tortilla?

Task 2

You are in a restaurant in Spain.
Your teacher will play the part of the waiter / waitress and will start the conversation.

1 Buenas tardes, ¿qué desea?

2 Por aquí. ¿Qué van a pedir?

3 Muy bien.

4 Sí. Y, ¿qué legumbres desean?

5 Muy bien. Y, ¿qué van a tomar?

Task 3

Write a letter to a Spanish pen-friend describing your tastes in food.

Use Notes/Options 2 and this Mind Map to help you.

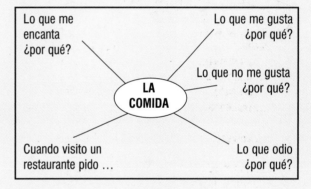

Lo que me encanta ¿por qué?

Lo que me gusta ¿por qué?

Lo que no me gusta ¿por qué?

LA COMIDA

Cuando visito un restaurante pido …

Lo que odio ¿por qué?

En el restaurante

checklist
What you need to know

Can you:

		Fine	Help!
1	do all the Foundation Checklist on page 71?	●	●

If you have ticked the Help! box, go back to the Foundation Checklist to revise.

2	respond to offers of food and drink, and give your reasons?	●	●
3	say how many there are in your group?	●	●
4	say exactly where you want to sit?	●	●
5	order your meal and change your order if something is not available?	●	●
6	Make complaints about a meal or service?	●	●

Eating out

Prepare a talk about food and dishes you like and dislike. Give opinions and reasons. Describe a recent meal in a restaurant. Use these Notes/Options below and the Mind Maps on page 122 to help you.

Help is at hand!

Notes/Options

1 *Only once you are really sure you are confident with the Foundation Checklist should you carry on with these Higher Notes/Options.*

2 ¿Quieres carne?

No, gracias. No como carne. Soy vegetariana.	= … I'm a vegetarian.
No como carne de vaca porque es contra mi religión.	= I don't eat beef because it's against my religion.
… carne de cerdo.	= … pork …
No me gusta el sabor.	= I don't like the flavour.
Tiene buen sabor.	
Sabe bien.	= It tastes good.
un poco	= a bit
un poco más	= a bit more
la mitad	= half
un pedazo pequeño	= a small slice
un mordisco.	= a bite
ya es bastante/ya basta	= that's enough
ya tengo bastante	= I've got enough
ya no más	= no more
¿Quieres más vino?	
No gracias. No quiero estár borracho/a.	= No thanks, I don't want to be drunk.
No quiero emborracharme.	= I don't want to get drunk.

3 ¿Cuántos son? = How many are there of you?

Somos cuatro adultos y un niño.

4 ¿Dónde se quieren sentar? = Where would you like to sit?

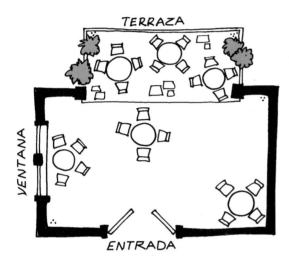

cerca de la ventana = by the window

lejos de la entrada = away from the entrance

en la terraza = on the terrace

en el rincón = in the corner

5 Lo siento, no queda pollo asado. = I'm sorry there is no roast chicken left.

Pues, ¿qué es el plato del día? = Well, what is the dish of the day?

chuletas de cerdo. = pork chops

Bueno, pues chuletas entonces. = Fine, chops, in that case.

6 No pedí guisantes. = I didn't order peas.

Pedímos hace media hora. = We ordered half an hour ago.

Oh, lo siento. = I'm sorry.

He estado esperando más de una hora. = I have been waiting for more than an hour.

En seguida. = Straight away.

¿Puede usted cambiarme este cuchillo? = Can you change my knife?

Le traigo un cuchillo limpio. = I'll bring you a clean knife.

Traíganos otro tenedor. = Bring us another fork.

Voy a traerles otro. = I'll bring you another.

Traígame … = Bring me …

No hay mostaza. = There is no mustard.

¿Hay libro de reclamaciones? = Is there a complaints book?

Tengo una queja. = I have a complaint.

See also Foundation Checklist 12 and 13.

Going for an A?

Make sure that you can talk about your food preferences. You should also be able to understand other people's opinions about food and drink. Be prepared to talk about a recent visit you have made to a restaurant either here or abroad.

Food and drink could come up in conversations about daily routine, and health and fitness. Check Chapters 2 and 3.

Test yourself

Task 1

Listen to the cassette twice (Side 1,
Chapter 8 Foundation).

Llamas por teléfono a un restaurante, El Río
de la Plata, en Málaga. He aquí la conversación.
Contesta 'sí' o 'no' a las preguntas siguientes:

	PREGUNTA	SI o NO
1	El restaurante está abierto a la una.	
2	Está abierto tres veces al día.	
3	Está cerrado los lunes todo el año.	
4	Tiene más de un menú turístico.	
5	Todos los menús tienen el mismo precio.	
6	Los padres son vegetarianos.	
7	El camarero no sabe que el jamón es carne.	
8	Los vegetarianos tienen dos posibilidades para el primer plato.	
9	No hay más de una clase de tortilla.	
10	El restaurante está situado bastante lejos de donde se aloja la familia.	

[10]

Task 2

You are with your friend at a restaurant
in Spain. You need to order something to
eat and drink for yourself and your friend and
find out what there is for dessert. Your friend
doesn't eat meat. Here is the menu.

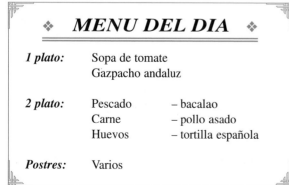

❖   MENU DEL DIA   ❖

1 plato:	Sopa de tomate	
	Gazpacho andaluz	
2 plato:	Pescado	– bacalao
	Carne	– pollo asado
	Huevos	– tortilla española
Postres:	Varios	

¿Si señor/señorita?

No queda tortilla. El pollo está muy bueno.

¿Y para beber?

Muy bien.

Hay flan y helado.

Task 3

Last year you stayed at the house of your
Spanish friend Sebastián. It was his
birthday while you were there. Write an account
of what you did on his birthday. The notes and
pictures below give an out line of events.

¿Qué hiciste?

¿Qué dijiste?

¿A dónde llamaste?

¿Por qué?

¿A qué hora llegaste al restaurante?

¿Dónde os sentasteis?

¿Qué pediste de primer plato? ¿Y tu compañero?

¿Y de segundo?

¿Y para beber?

¿Llegó a tiempo el primer plato?

¿Qué dijiste al camarero?

¿Qué contestó?

¿Te gustó la comida?

¿Pedisteis postre?

¿Café?

¿La cuenta?

¿La propina?

¿Como volvisteis a casa?

Give a clear progression through the events, using the past tenses. Add extra details if you can. Use the '-mas' ending on the verb to describe what you both did or had.

TAKE A BREAK

¡Enhorabuena! You have completed the chapter.

En el instituto

checklist
What you need to know

Can you:

	Fine	Help!
1 give details about your school: its size, type, number of pupils and facilities?	●	●
2 ask and talk about school routine: timetables, homework, breaks and games?	●	●
3 say how you travel to and from school?	●	●
4 say what subjects you like and why?	●	●
5 say what clubs and teams you belong to?	●	●
6 give simple opinions about your school?	●	●
7 say if you intend to leave or stay on at school?	●	●

At school

This topic is about you. Be prepared to talk and write about your school life in detail. Look at the Mind Maps on page 123 and make your own maps using the notes below to help you. Don't forget to follow the signposts for helpful hints.

Help is at hand!

Notes/Options

1 ¿Cómo se llama tu colegio / instituto?

Mi instituto se llama …

¿Cómo es tu colegio?

el instituto = secondary school
el colegio = high school or private school
la escuela = primary school

Es mixto.
… femenino
… masculino
… católico

= It's mixed.
= for girls
= for boys
= Catholic

¿Cómo son los edificios?
Son viejos.
… modernos.

edificios = buildings

Hay aulas (de lenguas, de inglés, ect.)	= There are classrooms (languages, English, etc.)
… laboratorios	= … labs
… laboratorio de lenguas	= … language labs
… campos de deportes	= … sports grounds
… canchas de tenis	= … tennis courts
… un gimnasio	= … gym
… un centro deportivo / polideportivo	= … sports centre
… patios	= … playgrounds
… biblioteca	= … library
… cantina	= … canteen
… el despacho del director / de la directora	= … the headmaster / mistress' office
… la secretaría	= … the secretary's office
… pasillos	= … corridors
… una sala de actos	= … hall

Make a mental note that clase = *lesson, and* aula = *classroom*

¿Cuántos alumnos hay? = How many pupils are there?

2 ¿En qué clase estás?

Estoy en cuarto. = I'm in the 4th year.
… quinto. = … 5th year.
… sexto. = … 6th year.

¿Cómo es tu horario? = What is your timetable like?

¿Qué asignaturas tienes el lunes por la mañana? = What subjects do you have on a Monday morning?

Los lunes tengo matemáticas de 9h 5 a 10h 20.

Después es el recreo. = Then it's break.

A las once menos veinte tengo ciencias. = At 10.40 I have science.

Antes de comer tengo educación física. = Before lunch I have P.E.

See the Mind Map on page 123 to revise school subjects.

¿A qué hora empieza el colegio? = What time does school start?

¿A qué hora empiezan las clases? = What time do lessons start?

Las clases empiezan a las 9h.

¿A qué hora termina el colegio? = What time does school finish?

¿Cuánto tiempo duran las clases? = How long do lessons last?

Duran 35 minutos.

¿A qué hora es el recreo? el recreo = break

¿Qué haces durante el recreo?

Charlo con mis amigos/as. = I chat with my friends.

Juego al fútbol.

Como algo. = I have something to eat.

Como un bocado. = I have a snack.

¿A qué hora es la comida? = What time is lunch?

¿Qué haces a mediodía? = What do you do at midday?

Paso la hora de comer en la cantina. = I spend the lunch hour in the canteen.

Traigo el almuerzo. = I bring a packed lunch.

Como la comida del colegio. = I have school dinners.

Vuelvo a casa a comer. = I go home for lunch.

¿Tienes muchos deberes? = Do you have a lot of homework?

Hago dos horas de deberes todas las tardes. = I have two hours of homework every evening.

¡Sí, tengo demasiados! = Yes, I have too much.

¿Qué deportes practicas en el instituto? = What sports do you do at school?

Juego al baloncesto y hago gimnasia.

See page 110 for other sports.

3 ¿Cómo vienes al colegio? = How do you come to school?

Vengo a pie. = I come on foot.

Voy andando. = I walk.

… en bici. = … by bike.

… en autobús. = … by bus.

Me trae mi padre en el coche. = My father brings me in the car.

9

Nunca llego tarde.	= I am never late.
A veces…	= sometimes …
Siempre …	= always

4 ¿Qué asignatura prefieres
y por qué?

Prefiero las ciencias porque
son útiles.

Me encanta el inglés porque
es fácil.

Me gustan las matemáticas
porque me gusta la profesora.

¿Qué asignatura no te gusta?
¿Por qué?

Odio la informática porque no estoy fuerte en esta asignatura.	soy fuerte = I'm good at
5 ¿Perteneces a algún club o esquipo escolar?	= Do you belong to any school club or team?
Sí, pertenezco al club de teatro.	= Yes, I belong to the theatre club.
Pertenezco al equipo de fútbol.	= I belong to the football team.

6 ¿Qué piensas de tu instituto?

Las clases son interesantes.

Las clases son aburridas.

Aprendo mucho.

No aprendo nada.

Los profesores son simpáticos.

7 ¿Qué vas a hacer después de los exámenes?	= What are you going to do after the exams?
¿Vas a dejar el colegio?	= Are you going to leave school?
¿Vas a dejar los estudios?	
Me quedaré en el instituto para aprobar mis 'A' levels.	= I'm going to stay at school to get my 'A' levels.
Dejaré de estudiar.	= I'll stop studying.
Depende de los resultados.	

Going for a C?

Be prepared to talk about what you did at school yesterday.

Ayer	=	Yesterday
tuve un examen	=	I had an exam.
estudié …	=	I studied …
trabajé …	=	I worked …
vine al colegio …	=	I came to school …
comí …	=	I ate …
llegué …	=	I arrived …
salí …	=	I left …

Be prepared to talk about your last report and your estimated grades.

mis notas	= my report
Saqué un notable en geografía.	= I got an A / a 'very good' in geography.
Voy a sacar …	= I'm going to get …
sobresaliente	= excellent
bien	= good
suficiente	= satisfactory
insuficiente	= poor
muy deficiente	= very poor
voy a suspender …	= I am going to fail in …
saco buenas notas en …	= I get good marks in …

Test yourself

Task 1

Listen to the cassette (Side 1, Chapter 9, Foundation). Play the cassette twice.

	LUNES	MARTES	MIÉRCOLES	JUEVES	VIERNES
9–10					
10–11					
11–11.30	RECREO	RECREO	RECREO	RECREO	RECREO
11.30–12.30					
12.30–1.30					
1.30–4	ALMUERZO	ALMUERZO	ALMUERZO	ALMUERZO	ALMUERZO
4–5					
5–6					

Recibes este cassette con más información sobre un instituto español. En el horario pon una **E** cuando hay una clase de español y pon una **I** cuando hay una clase de inglés.

(7 marks)

Un Año Escolar en un Colegio Inglés

La organización internacional, EF, ofrece un programa especial para estudiantes españoles que quieren pasar un año entero estudiando en Inglaterra. El programa consiste en:

– Alojamiento con una familia inglesa.
– Clases normales en un colegio inglés.
– Viaje de ida y vuelta en avión.

Tu colegio participa en este programa, y en setiembre un estudiante español que se llama Jaime va a llegar para vivir 9 meses con tu familia. Va a ir a tu colegio también. Escribe una carta a Jaime, incluyendo la información siguiente:

Debes escribir unas 100 palabras.

- información sobre las personas en tu familia;

- información sobre tu colegio;

- las asignaturas que estudias y tus opiniones sobre ellas;

- cómo son tus profesores;

- tus pasatiempos preferidos.

As well as using the Notes/Options from this Chapter, use those in Chapters 3 and 4 to help you cover the first and final point.

Answers

TASK 1

E = lunes 10–11, miércoles 5–6, viernes 4–5 + 5–6;
I = viernes 9–10, martes 11.30–12.30, jueves 11.30–12.30.

TAKE A BREAK

En el instituto

checklist
What you need to know

Can you:

	Fine	Help!
1 complete the Foundation Checklist on page 80?	○	○

If you have ticked the Help! box, go back to the Foundation Notes/Options and revise.

2 say how long you have been learning Spanish and any other foreign languages?	○	○
3 talk about your timetable, terms and holidays?	○	○
4 discuss school subjects, rules and uniform?	○	○
5 say which exams you are taking and discuss your future plans at school?	○	○
6 describe special events and trips in the school year?	○	○

At school

Use a variety of tenses to talk about school trips and ambition. Give examples where possible. Say why you have decided on your future plans. Be prepared to compare your school routine with one in a Spanish-speaking country. Use the Notes/Options below as models to prepare a talk on this topic.

Help is at hand!

Notes/Options

1 *Only once you are really sure you are confident with the Foundation Checklist should you carry on with these Higher Notes/Options.*

2 ¿Cuánto tiempo llevas aprendiendo el español? = How long have you been learning Spanish?

Llevo cinco años aprendiendo el español. = I have been learning Spanish for five years.

¿Hablas otros idiomas? = Do you speak any other languages?

Hablo portugues, italiano, gujarati …

3 *See Chapter 6, Foundation Checklist 1.*

¿Crees que tienes suficientes vacaciones? = Do you think you have enough holidays?

¡Qué va! = No way!

En España las vacaciones de verano empiezan antes. = The summer holidays start earlier.

Las vacaciones de verano son más largas. = The holidays are longer.

Hay más días de fiesta oficiales. = There are more bank holidays.

… la vacación de Semana Santa es muy corta. = … the Easter holiday is very short.

… no hay vacaciones a mitad del trimestre. = … there are no half-term holidays.

Si las vacaciones fueran más largas me aburriría. = If the holidays were longer I would get bored.

4 ¿Cómo es tu horario?

	= What is your timetable like?
Está cargado.	= It's full / loaded.
Está bien equilibrado.	= It's well balanced.
Estudio diez asignaturas.	= I do ten subjects.
Ciertas asignaturas son obligatorias.	= Some subjects are compulsory.
He elegido ciertas asignaturas.	= I have chosen certain subjects.
Hay opciones.	= There are options.

Be prepared to talk about what you do on your favourite and least favourite day, and say why you like or dislike that day.

Learn the following reasons for liking and disliking subjects, school and uniform.

Las asignaturas	= The subjects
Siempre saco buenas notas.	= I always get good marks.
Nunca saco buenas notas.	= I never get good marks.
Siempre apruebo los exámenes.	= I always pass my exams.
Siempre suspendo los exámenes.	= I always fail my exams.
Nunca tengo que repetir los exámenes.	= I never have to re-take my exams.
Tengo que repetir.	= I have to retake my exams.
Encuentro el trabajo fácil.	= I find the work easy.
Encuentro el trabajo difícil.	= I find the work difficult.
El profesor explica bien la asignatura.	= The teacher explains the subject well.
La profesora no explica la materia.	= The teacher doesn't explain the subject properly.
El profesor es divertido.	= The teacher is fun.
La profesora no es simpática.	= The teacher is not friendly.
El profesor no nos da demasiados deberes.	= The teacher doesn't give us too much homework.
La profesora nos da demasiados deberes.	= The teacher gives us too much homework.

La disciplina	= Discipline
Los profesores son estrictos / severos pero no demasiado.	= The teachers are strict but not too strict.
Los profesores son demasiado estrictos.	= The teachers are too strict.
Hay buen ambiente.	= There is a good atmosphere.
Hay mal ambiente.	= There is a bad atmosphere.
No es muy ruidoso.	= It's not too noisy.
Es muy ruidoso.	= It's very noisy.
Los alumnos se portan bien.	= The pupils behave well.
Los alumnos se portan mal.	= The pupils behave badly.

El uniforme	= Uniform
No tengo que elegir lo que ponerme por la mañana.	= I don't have to choose what to wear every morning.
Quiero elegir lo que ponerme todos los días.	= I want to choose what I wear everyday.
Es práctico.	= It's practical.
Es incómodo.	= It's uncomfortable.
Me gusta el estilo.	= I like the style.
No está de moda.	= It's not fashionable.

5 ¿De qué exáminarás este verano?

Me exáminaré al nivel GCSE en dibujo, en español ..	= I'm taking GCSE exams in …

Don't forget to pronounce the initials of GCSE in Spanish: **heh, theh, ese, eh.**

Espero aprobar los exámenes.	= I hope to pass my exams.
Espero no suspender.	= I'm hoping not to fail.
Si apruebo espero continuar con mis estudios.	= If I pass I hope to carry on with my studies.
Quiero trabajar.	= I want to work.
Quiero un empleo.	= I want a job.

6 Durante el año escolar hay obras de teatro. = During the school year there are plays.

… espectáculos. = … shows.

… conciertos. = … concerts.

… un día de competiciones deportivas. = … sports day.

… reuniones para los padres y los profesores. = … parents' evenings.

… partidos de baloncesto. = … basketball matches.

… excursiones escolares. = … school trips.

… intercambios escolares. = … school exchanges.

Test yourself

Task 1

Listen to the cassette (Side 1, Chapter 9, Higher).

Three Spaniards are talking about school. Put a ✔ in the correct space to indicate the appropriate person.

Here is an example.

	Antonio	Paco	Reyes
			✔

Who goes home to lunch?
The answer is Reyes.

Now read questions 1 – 4 and hear the cassette.

	Antonio	Paco	Reyes
1 Who likes going to school?			
2 Who does not like French?			
3 Who does not attend all his/her classes?			
4 Who says that they like their holidays?			

Going for an A?

Be prepared to talk about what normally happens at these events. Use Generalmente, normalmente, de costumbre + the present tense.

Normalmente	se invitan a los padres…
Generalmente	hay que pagar la entrada…
De costumbre	los alumnos preparan …
Siempre	se dan premios…
	se publica una revista…

Be prepared to talk about these events last year. Use El año pasado + the preterite tense (see the Mind Map on page 126).

El año pasado estuve en el reparto	= I was in the cast
hize el papel de …	= I played the part of…
toqué en la orquestra	= I played in the orchestra
participé en el concurso	= I took part in the competition
jugué en el equipo	= I played in the team
repasé las materias	= I revised

Be prepared to talk about school life and routine in Spain as well as your own school experiences. Make comparisons. You might find the Mind Maps on page 123 useful for this.

En España hay **más** vacaciones **que** en el Reino Unido.

En el Reino Unido el descanso para comer es **menos** largo **que** en España.

Task 2

Prepara un cassette grabado en español. Debes hablar durante tres o cuatro minutos sobre tu colegio y tu vida escolar.

Mention the size, description, type and location of your school, and describe your routine there. Talk about your school subjects and preferences, as well as extra-curricular activities. Remember to mention what subjects you are doing now, and what you will be doing from next September. Wherever you can, give an opinion and your reasons.

Task 3

Abacas de pasar una semana en un colegio español. Tienes que escribir un artículo para la revista del colegio español, dando tus impresiones y comparándolo con tu propio colegio. Escribe aproximadamente 150 palabras.

Hiciste estas notas:

La vida escolar

- Mañana: clases de 9h 00 a 12h 30, con recreo de 30 minutos.

- Comida: no hay cantina. Los chicos van a casa.

- Tarde: clases de 16h 00 a 18h 00.

- Dos horas de deberes al día.

- Jueves tarde: no hay clase.

- Sábado mañana: hay clase.

- Vacaciones de verano: desde finales de junio hasta septiembre.

- Dos semanas de vacaciones en Navidad, y dos en Semana Santa.

---

[20]

Task 4

Lee esta carta.

... En el instituto estudio matemáticas, informática, geografía, historia, lengua española, química, física, inglés, alemán y dibujo. Saco buenas notas en idiomas, informática y matemáticas pero encuentro difíciles las ciencias. Me gustan los deportes y soy miembro del equipo de baloncesto. Tenemos partidos cada dos semanas contra equipos de otros institutos de la región.

Rellena los detalles EN ESPAÑOL:

Idioma(s) estudiado(s):	
Asignatura(s) fuerte(s):	
Asignatura(s) floja(s):	
Deportes:	

Answers

TASK 1

1 Paco **2** Antonio **3** Antonio **4** Reyes

TASK 4

1 Español, alemán, inglés (any 2 = 1 mark each)

2 Lenguas, informática, matemáticas (any 2 = 1 mark each)

3 Ciencias (1)

4 Baloncesto

TAKE A BREAK

¡Enhorabuena! You have completed the chapter!

En el trabajo

checklist
What you need to know

Can you:

	Fine	Help!

Work

1 give information about future work plans?

2 give information about how you get to work and how long it takes?

3 say that someone is out of work?

4 understand details about jobs, including weekend jobs and work experience?

5 say if you have a job in your spare time and give information about it, such as hours and pay?

6 give simple opinions about jobs?

7 say which jobs you and your family do?

Advertising

8 understand and give simple opinions about adverts?

Communication

9 ask and give a phone number and answer a phone call, saying who you are?

10 ask to speak to someone and take or leave a message?

At work

Being able to express opinions is a major consideration for this topic. Check the Notes/Options below to help you express your opinions in Spanish. Make sure you know what to say when you pick up a phone in Spanish! Use the Mind Maps for this chapter to revise the vocabulary you need to talk about jobs. Be sure you know how to say what jobs the members of your family have.

Help is at hand!

Notes/Options

1 ¿Qué quieres hacer en el futuro?	= What do you want to do in the future?
¿Qué quieres ser?	= What do you want to be?
¿Qué carrera … ?	carrera = profession
¿Qué profesión …?	profesión = job / profession
¿Qué empleo…?	empleo = job / employment
Quiero ser abogado.	= I want to be a lawyer.
Pienso ser actor / actriz.	= I intend being an actor / actress.
Espero ser arquitecto.	= I hope to be an architect.

Quiero trabajar con ordenadores.	= I want to work in computers.	Sí, es un/a …	
Quiero tener una carrera / un trabajo / un puesto en negocios.	= I want a profession / job / post in business.	No, está en paro.	= He / She is unemployed.

… en la industría.
… en la medicina.
… en el servicio diplomático.
… en relaciones públicas.

Está parado.

Quiero ganarme la vida trabajando con animales.	= I want to earn a living working with animals.

4 *Useful phrases which you need to understand:*

Las horas de trabajo son de 9h a 5h.	= The working hours are from 9 to 5 o'clock.
el día laborable	= the working day
Se necesita: Funcionario	= Wanted: Administrator
Se requiere: Director	= Wanted: Manager
Se pide: Jefe de Obras	= Wanted: Site Manager
Precisa: Consultores	= Wanted: Consultants
Solicita: Técnico	= Wanted: Technician
Se ofrece salario a convenir	= Salary negotiable
Se valora experiencia mínima	= Minimal experience appreciated
Requisitos	= requirements
Funciones	= duties
Formación	= training
Los interesados deben enviar su C.V. actualizado.	= Candidates should send a current C.V.
salario / sueldo	= salary

Quiero un trabajo interesante.

Espero continuar / seguir mis estudios.	= I hope to carry on studying.

Voy a ir a la universidad.

Quiero una carrera.	= I want a profession.
Voy a buscar trabajo.	= I'm going to look for a job.
Voy a hacer un curso de formación profesional.	= I'm going to do a training course.
… un curso de informática.	= … a computer course.
… un aprenizaje.	= … an apprenticeship.
No he decidido todavía.	= I haven't decided yet.
Depende en si apruebo los exámenes.	= It depends on my exam results.

Make sure you can say what your future plans are. Look at the Mind Map on page 124 for ideas.

Work experience

hacer prácticas laborales / profesionales	= to do work experience
Hice mis prácticas laborales en + name of firm / organisation.	= I did my work experience at …
Hice dos semanas de prácticas laborales.	= I did two weeks of work experience.
Tenía que archivar.	= I had to do filing.
… contestar el teléfono.	= … answer the phone.
… trabajar en una obra.	= … work on a building site.

2 ¿Cómo vas a trabajar? = How do you go to work?

See Chapter 6, Foundation Notes/Options 7.

El viaje dura tres cuartos de hora.	= The journey takes 45 minutes ($\frac{3}{4}$ of hour).

3 ¿Trabaja tu padre / madre / hermano / hermana? = Does your father / mother / brother / sister work?

5 ¿Trabajas? = Do you work?

¿Tienes un trabajo / empleo? = Do you have a job?

Sí, trabajo en un supermercado.	= Yes, I work in a supermarket.
… en una tienda.	= … in a shop.
… en una hamburguesería.	= … in a hamburger restaurant.
… en una peluquería.	= … in a hairdresser's.
Reparto periódicos.	= I have a paper round.
Hago de canguro.	= I do baby-sitting.
No, no trabajo.	= No, I don't work.

Trabajo los sábados.	= I work on Saturdays.
… todas las tardes.	= … every evening.
… dos tardes a la semana.	= … two evenings a week.
¿Está bien pagado?	= Is it well paid?
No está mal. Recibo tres libras por hora.	= Not bad. I get £3 an hour.
… veinte libras al día.	= … £20 a day.
No, está mal pagado.	= It's badly paid.
Paga mal.	= It pays badly.

See Chapter 4 Notes/Options 11 for useful phrases to describe what you spend your money on.

6 ¿Qué piensas de tu trabajo? What do you think of your job?

Es interesante.
Es aburrido.
Me gusta trabajar con el público. = I like to work with people
Me cansa. = I get tired.
Es variado.
Es repetitivo.
Mis compañeros son simpáticos.
No me llevo bien con mis compañeros. = I don't get on with my workmates.

7 Look at the Mind Maps on page 124.

8 la publicidad = advertising

en mi opinion …	= in my opinion …
el anuncio	= advert
la cartelera	= bill board
el póster	= poster
Los anuncios en la tele son muy entretenidos.	= TV ads. are very entertaining.
No los tomo en serio.	= I don't take them seriously.
Tienen mucha imaginación.	= They are very imaginative.
No representan la realidad.	= They don't represent real life.
Mucha gente los toma en serio.	= Lots of people taken them seriously.
Influyen demasiado a la gente.	= They influence people too much.

9/10 *See Chapter 7 Foundation Notes/Options 19 for how to give and ask for a phone number.*

¿Diga?

¿Dígame?

See Chapter 8 Foundation Notes/Options 19 for how to leave a message.

¿Quieres dejar un recado / un mensaje?	= Do you want to leave a message?
Sí, de parte de Marcos.	= Yes, it's Marcos.
¿Puedo volver a llamar dentro de media hora?	= Can I phone back in half an hour?
Puede volver a llamar.	= You can ring back.
No cuelgue.	= Don't hang up.
Está comunicando.	= It's engaged.
Marque otra vez.	= Dial again.

¿Diga? = Hello?

Going for a C?

How much can you understand of this advert for training courses? Use a dictionary if you get stuck.

Con CEAC, SÍ puedes aprender.

Curso de Esteticista

Aprendes en casa, a tu ritmo, sin horarios ni desplazamientos.

Tendrás un profesor al teléfono que resolverá todas tus dudas.

Con todo el material necesario, para que puedas practicar desde el primer día.

Conseguirás tu diploma CEAC que acreditará tus conocimientos y profesionalidad.

Con la garantía CEAC: si al terminar el curso no estás satisfecho, te reembolsaremos el dinero abonado.

Con una institución con 50 años de experiencia. Más de un millón y medio de alumnos han aprendido con CEAC.

CEAC

En vanguardia desde 1946

902 102 103

Servicio de información 24h.

Test yourself

Task 1

Listen to the cassette (Side 1, Chapter 10 Foundation).

MENSAJE POR CONTESTADOR AUTOMATICO

Answer the following questions **in English**.

Your friend's father does not speak Spanish, so you offer to listen to the message in Spanish on his ansaphone

1 Where is Marcos ringing from?

2 How will he get to central London?

3 a What time does the train leave London?

　 b What time will he arrive?

4 a How does he hope to get from the station to your house?

　 b When will he telephone again?

5 What will he bring with him? Give details.

Task 2

You have an interview for a summer job as a waiter/waitress in a holiday resort in Spain. Can you answer the following questions?

¿Buscas un empleo?

¿Qué empleo has escogido?

¿Cómo te llamas?

¿Cuántos años tienes?

¿Dónde vives?

¿Cuál es tu dirección exacta?

¿Cuál es tu número de teléfono?

Háblame un poco de tu familia.

Describe tu carácter.

¿Qué asignaturas estudias en el colegio?

¿Cuándo vas a salir del colegio?

¿Cuándo puedes empezar a trabajar? ¿En qué fecha?

Task 3

Subraya la palabra adecuada.

Ejemplo: Marisol es camarera / <u>dependienta</u> / pintora.

OFERTAS
BOLSA DE TRABAJO

Dependienta con experiencia se ofrece para trabajar fines de semana.
Teléfono 981/224184 – Marisol

Se dan clases particulares de inglés. Llamar tardes.
José
Telef. 282550

Se ofrece chica de 19 años con buenas referencias para cuidar niños, o para limpieza. Carmen. Teléfono 290362.

Jardinero se ofrece para trabajar 10 horas por semana. Pepe. Tlf. 287975.

Busco trabajo como camarero de 16.00 a 20.00 solamente. Ramón. 293264.

A Marisol puede trabajar los lunes / jueves / sábados.

B José es profesor / chófer / policía.

C Carmen quiere trabajar con chicas / niños / clientes.

D Pepe quiere trabajar siete / seis / diez horas por semana.

E Ramón quiere trabajar por la mañana / tarde / noche.

[5]

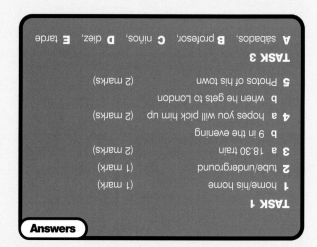

Answers

TASK 1
1 home/his home   (1 mark)
2 tube/underground   (1 mark)
3 a 18.30 train   (2 marks)
   b 9 in the evening
4 a hopes you will pick him up   (2 marks)
   b when he gets to London
5 Photos of his town   (2 marks)

TASK 3
A sábados, **B** profesor, **C** niños, **D** diez, **E** tarde

10

En el trabajo

At work

Prepare a talk on your work experience or spare-time job (if you have one). Give details about hours, pay, whether you like it or not and why. Prepare another one on the job you hope to have in the future. Give as many details as possible. Make sure you know how to make enquires. Model your answers on the Notes/Options below and use the Mind Maps on page 124 to revise the vocabulary for this topic.

Help is at hand!

Notes/Options

1 *Only once you are really sure you are confident with the Foundation Checklist should you carry on with these Higher Notes/Options.*

2/3

¿Qué harás después del colegio?	= What will you do when you leave school?
¿Qué carrera quieres tener?	= What career do you want to follow?
¿Qué quieres hacer en el futuro?	= What do you want to do in the future?

Quiero ser	porque
profesor/a	me gusta la enseñanza
periodista	me apasiona la actualidad
niñero/a	adoro a los niños
médico	quiero ayudar a la gente
veterinario	quiero trabajar con animales
contable	se me dan bien las cifras
intérprete	me gusta hablar diferentes idiomas
albañil	voy a trabajar con mi padre
hombre/mujer de negocios	quiero ganar mucho dinero
instructor/a de educación física	me obsesiona estar en forma
granjero	quiero trabajar al aire libre
abogado	me interesa el derecho

checklist
What you need to know

Can you:

		Fine	Help!
1	Foundation Checklist on page 88?		

If you have ticked the Help! box go back and revise.

2	give reasons for your choice of study or job?		
3	express hopes about your future plans after studying?		
4	give details about jobs, weekend jobs and work experience?		
5	understand and give opinions about different jobs?		
6	make arrangements to be contacted by phone or fax?		
7	ask what work others do?		
8	enquire about the availability of work?		

Leave out the un/a *when talking about what you want to be.*

Quiero hacer un curso de programador de ordenadores.	= I want to do a computer programming course.

Quiero continuar mis estudios.

Quiero seguir estudiando.

Quiero ir a la universidad.

Quiero tener una carrera universitaria.

Quiero ser licienciado/a.	= I want to graduate.
Quiero tener un título.	= I want to get a degree.
Quiero tener éxito en la vida.	= I want to be successful.
Quiero ganarme la vida de manera útil.	= I want to earn my living in a useful way.
¿Qué calificaciones necesitas?	= What qualifications do you need?
Tienes que hacer un curso de estudios superiores para ser...	= You have to do further studies to be a ...
Tengo pensado ser ...	
Espero ser ...	= I hope to be a ...
Ya veremos.	= We'll see.

4 *See Foundation Notes/Options 4 for phrases to describe jobs. Make sure you can say and write those phrases.*

5 Tus opiniones sobre los empleos

Ventajas = Pros	Desventajas = Cons
Está bien pagado.	Está mal pagado
El sueldo es alto.	El sueldo es bajo
Se puede vivir en / viajar al extranjero.	
	Es duro.
Hay posibilidades de ascenso. = There are promotion prospects.	Es estresante. = It is stressful.

6 Quisiera enviar un fax.	= I'd like to send a fax.
Quiero enviar este documento por fax.	= I'd like to fax this document.
Atención de ...	= For the attention of ...
Me puede contactar por fax en el 00266456.	
Respóndame por fax.	= Fax me a reply.
Deje un recado en el contestador automático.	= Leave a message on the answering machine.
Juan Polaco al aparato.	= Juan Polaco speaking.
No cuelgue usted.	= Don't hang up.
7 ¿En qué trabaja usted?	*Used to somebody you do not know well.*
¿Qué profesión tiene usted?	
8 Solicitando trabajo	= Applying for work

Test yourself

Task 1

Listen to the cassette (Side 1, Chapter 10, Higher). Play the cassette twice.

You hear these young people talking on the radio and your friend wants to know what the programme is about.

1 How do you explain Javier's interest in television cartoons?

2 a What is Cristina's ambition?

  b How is she preparing for it?

3 Why does Virginia worry that she may not fulfil her ambition?

4 a What type of work experience is Manolo gaining?

  b What often makes Manolo's job difficult?

5 Why does Cecilia seem to have a rather unrealistic ambition?

6 What does Roberto do to relax?

Going for an A?

Learn the phrases highlighted in this letter.

Sra. Juana Ramírez, Jefe de Personal
Grandes almacenes Puig
Barcelona.

Muy Sra. mía:

Ref: Dependienta

En relación con el anuncio[1] **aparecido en el diario**[2] El correo de Catalunya **de fecha**[3] 6 de abril, **deseo solicitar la plaza de**[4] dependienta.

Tengo experiencia en este tipo de trabajo[5]. **Trabajé**[6] como dependienta unos dos meses en unos grandes almacenes en Birmingham el verano pasado. **En estos momentos soy**[7] estudiante de idiomas. . **Llevo estudiando el español por seis años**[8]. **También tengo conocimientos de francés**[9].

Desde 1986 **hasta** 1991 **asistí a la Escuela Primaria.**[10] **Los estudios secundarios los hago en**[11] Birmingham y **espero obtener**[12] mis Certificados de Educación General Secundaria en agosto de este año.

Estaré libre para empezar a trabajar desde el 1 de junio **hasta** el 2 de septiempre.[13]

Mando ajunto mi C.V. [14] y **referencias escritas por** mi profesora de español[15]

Le agradecería si me enviase más informacion sobre el trabajo sobre el sueldo y las horas laborales[16].

En espera de sus noticias[17] **le saluda atentamente**[18],

Debbie Bridgeman

1. With regard to the advertisement
2. Which appeared in the … paper
3. dated …
4. I would like to apply for the position of …
5. I have experience in this type of work
6. I worked …
7. At this moment in time I am …
8. I have been learning Spanish for 6 years
9. I also have knowledge of French
10. From … to … I attended primary school
11. I attend secondary school in …
12. I hope to obtain …
13. I will be available to start work from … to …
14. I enclose my C.V.
15. and references from …
16. I would be grateful if you could send me more information about the job, with respect to wages and working hours.
17. Looking forward to your reply
18. Yours sincerely …

Task 2

Imagine you are being interviewed for the job of dependienta. Can you answer the following questions?

1 ¿Tienes un empleo en estos momentos?

2 ¿Desde hace cuánto tiempo trabajas?

3 ¿Por qué quieres trabajar en España?

4 ¿Has estado ya alguna vez en España?

5 ¿Cuándo? ¿Durante cuánto tiempo? ¿Con quién?

6 ¿Qué piensas de este empleo? ¿Por qué lo has escogido?

7 ¿Qué harás después del colegio?

8 ¿Tienes alguna pregunta?

Task 3

You read this article about the tennis star Arancha Sánchez.

¡¡Vamos, Arancha, vamos!!

Pasión por el tenis
Arancha (Aránzazu) Sánchez-Vicario nació el 18 de diciembre de 1971 en Barcelona. **A los cuatro años empezó a jugar al tenis.**

¿Empezaste a jugar al tenis porque te daban envidia tus hermanos?
No exactemente envidia. Pero desde los tres años yo veía todo el tiempo por mi casa raquetas y pelotas. Yo quería hacer lo mismo que hacían los mayores. Así que desde muy pequeña he estado casi más con la raqueta que con las muñecas.

¿Te resultaba difícil compaginar el tenis con el cole?
La verdad es que sí era un poco difícil. Pero había que hacerlo, porque el cole era también muy importante.
Antes estudiaba por correspondencia, pero cada vez era más difícil, porque este deporte te exige estar siempre a tope si quieres estar entre las mejores. Así que lo dejé en segundo de BUP.

¿Qué te gusta hacer cuando no estás en una competición o entrenando?
Me gusta mucho leer. Casi de todo: historia, novelas … También me encanta escuchar música, y poder estar tranquilamente con mis amigos. Y, por supuesto, estar en casa con mi familia y con mis dos perros.

Dinos tu sueño.
(No lo duda ni un momento.) Una medalla olímpica.
Seguir mejorando y llegar a ser la número uno del mundo.

A friend wants to know more about her and asks you to fill in the missing details on this form.

Name Arancha Sánchez

Date and place of birth 18th December 1971, Barcelona

At what age did she start playing tennis?
When she was four years old

Why?

(a) _____

Why did she stop studying?

(b) _____

Pastimes? (i) Reading

(ii) Listening to music

(c)   (iii) _____

What are her plans for the future?

(i) Win an olympic medal

(d)   (ii) _____

Task 4

Quieres ir a España este verano pero no tienes dinero. Buscas un trabajo en España. En un periódico español, ves este anuncio.

> Necesito estudiantes ingleses para trabajar en hoteles durante el verano
>
> Se exige ………… buena salud
> idiomas extranjeros
> buenas referencias
>
> Escribe con detalles a:
> Sr Moreno
> Calle Goya 4-3-A
> Madrid

Escribe una carta de unas 100 palabras al Sr. Morales. Incluye la información siguiente:-

– información personal, edad, ect;

– tus estudios de español y otros idiomas;

– tu experiencia en otros trabajos que has hecho;

– preguntas sobre el trabajo en el hotel (por ejemplo, dinero, horas …);

– las fechas en que puedes trabajar.

Use Notes/Options 8 to help you.

A Mind Map to summarise these colour pages

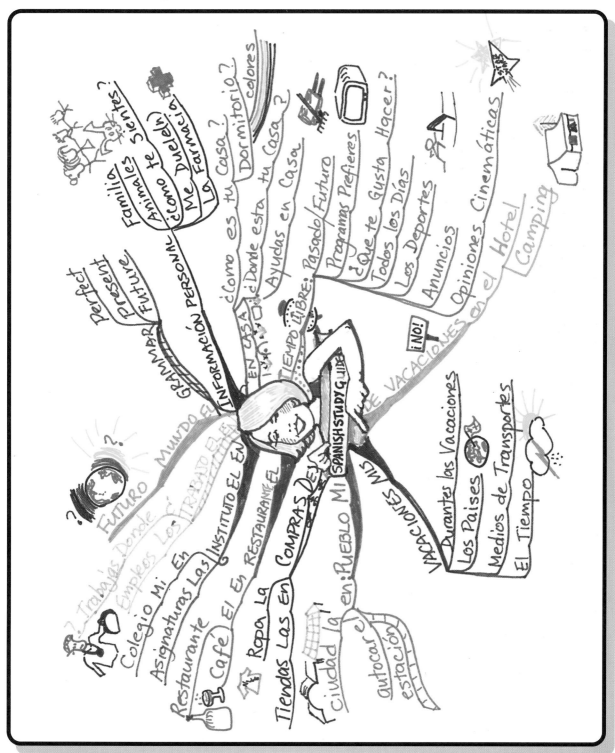

1 Información personal

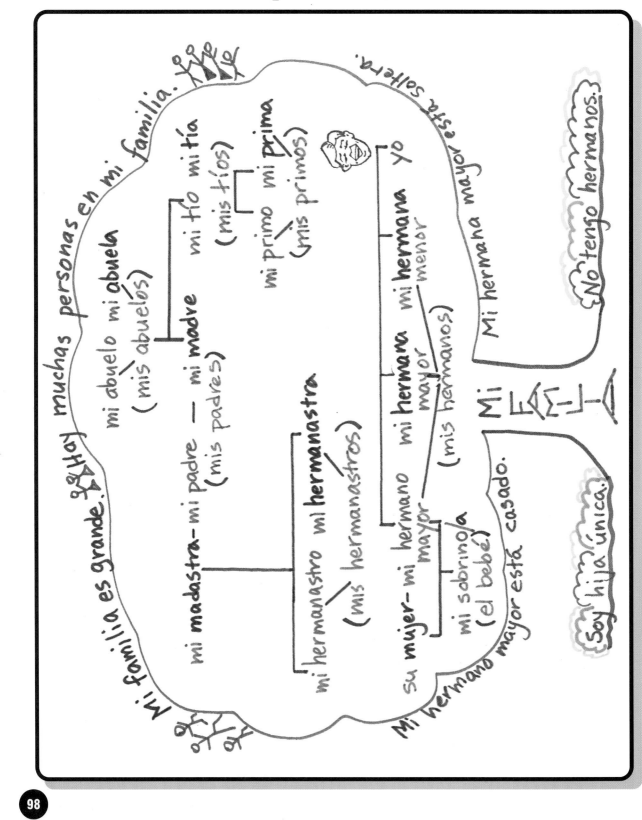

Mi familia es grande. ¡Hay muchas personas en mi familia.

mi abuelo   mi abuela
(mis abuelos)

mi tío   mi tía
(mis tíos)

mi padre — mi madre
(mis padres)

mi primo   mi prima
(mis primos)

Yo

mi madrastra — mi hermanastro   mi hermanastra
(mis hermanastros)

su mujer — mi hermano   mi hermana   mi hermana
mayor   mayor
menor
(mis hermanos)

Mi hermano mayor está casado.

mi sobrino/a
(el bebé)

Mi hermana mayor está soltera.

No tengo hermanos.

Mi FAMILIA

Soy hija única.

1 Información personal

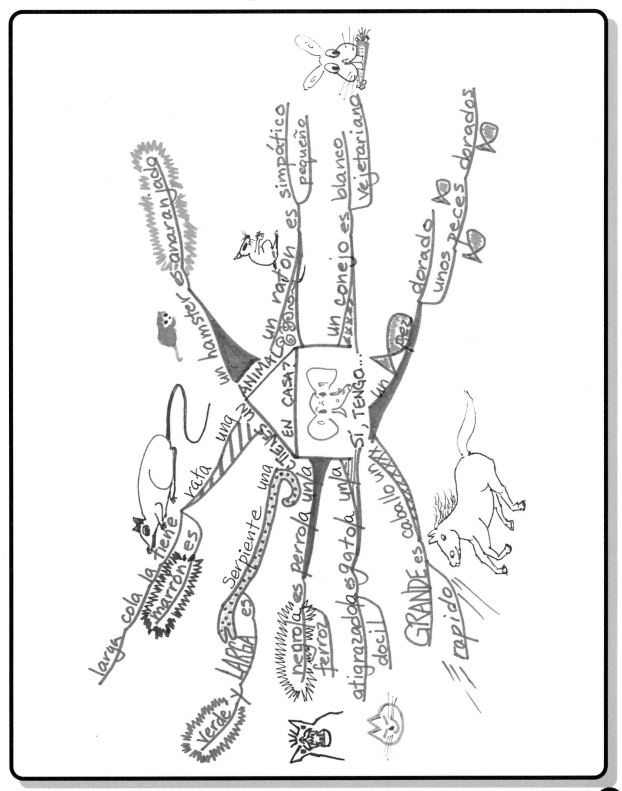

1 Información personal

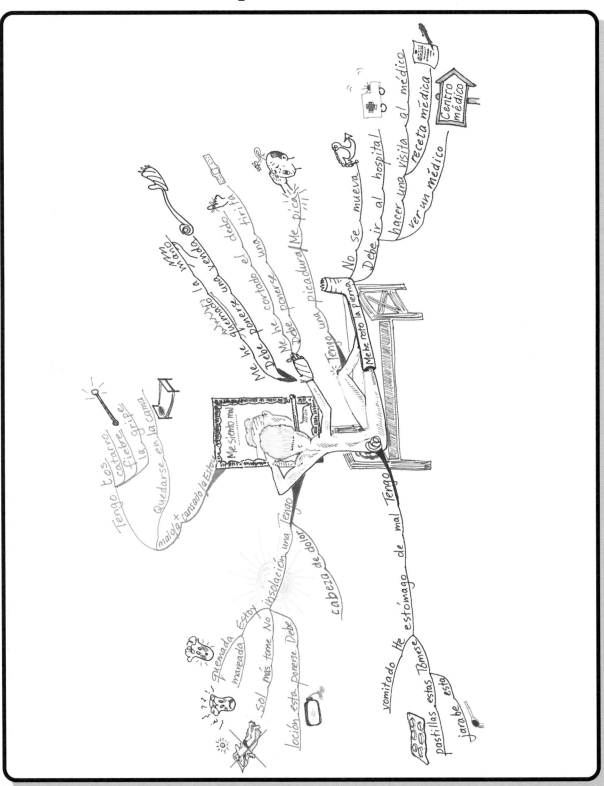

1 Información personal

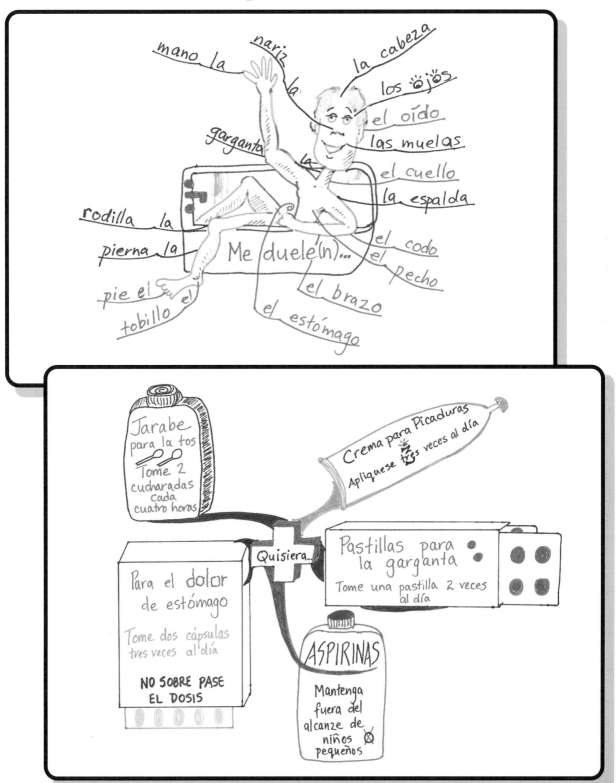

2 En casa

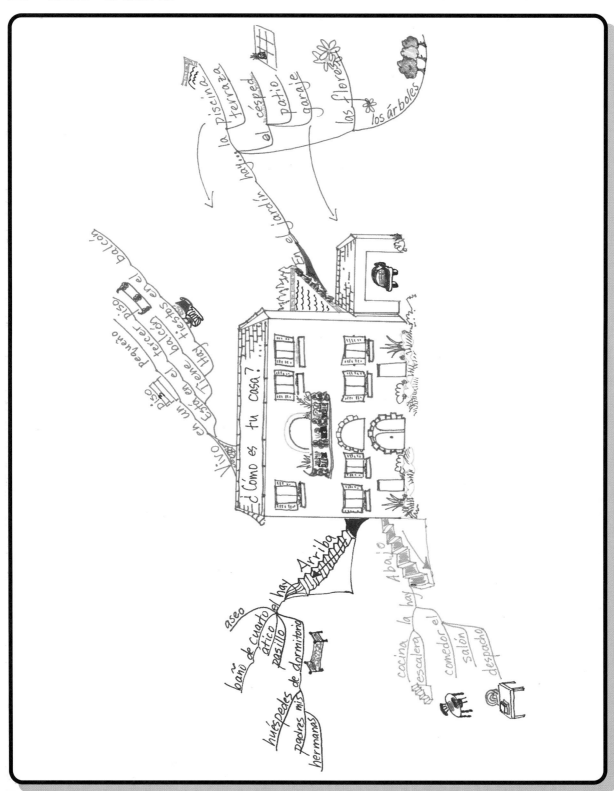

2 En casa

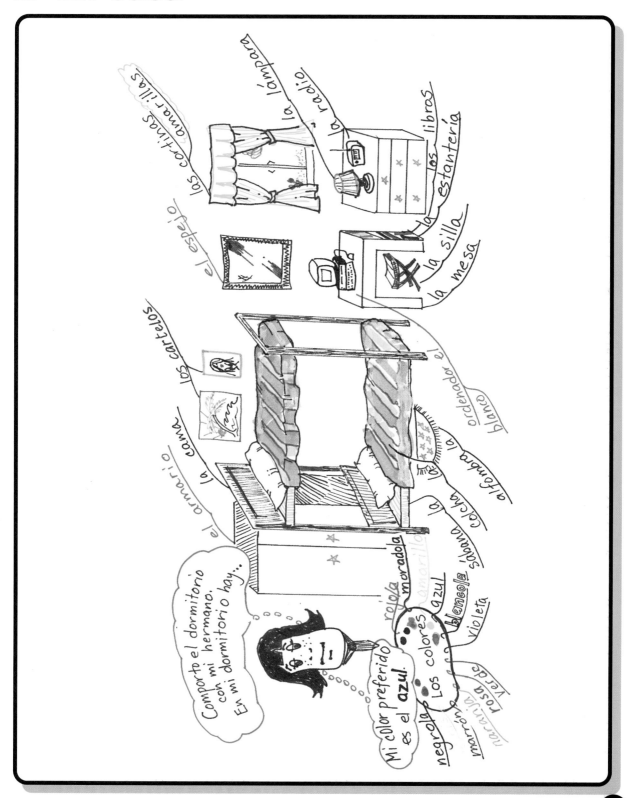

2 En casa

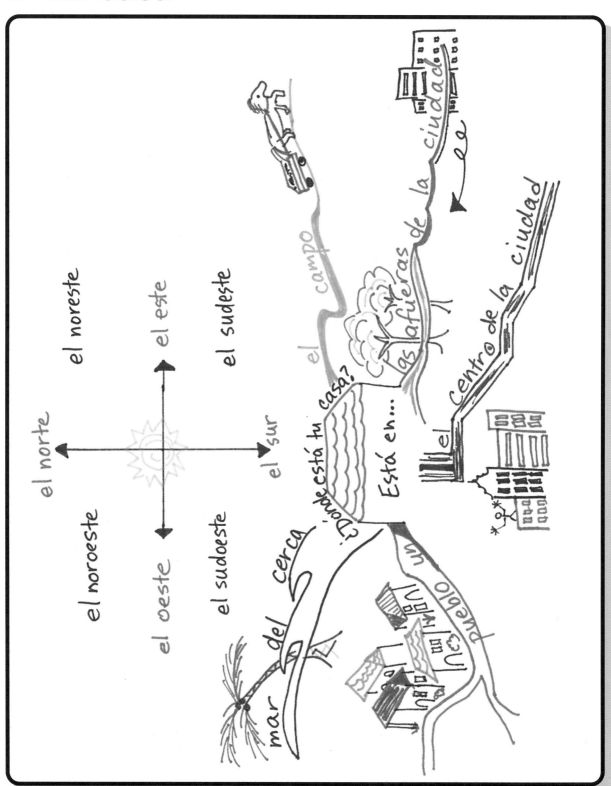

2 En casa

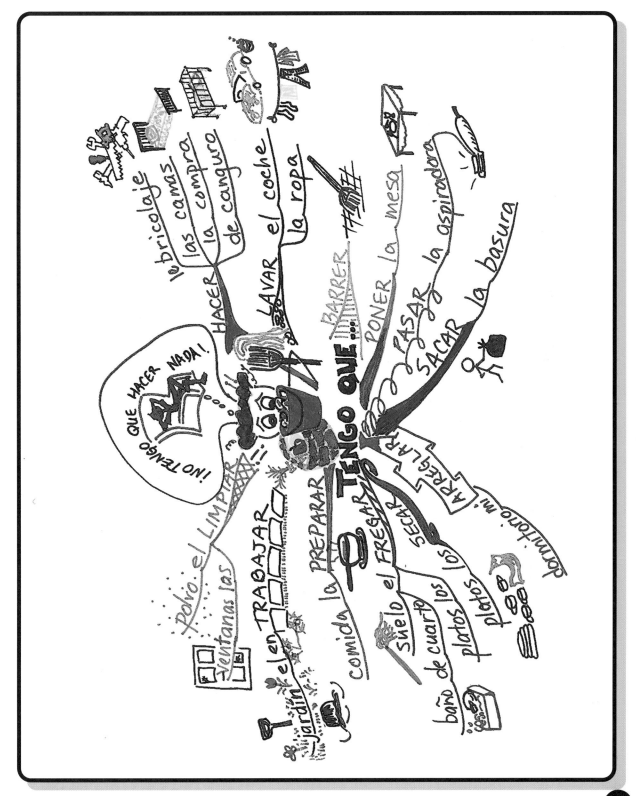

3 En mi tiempo libre

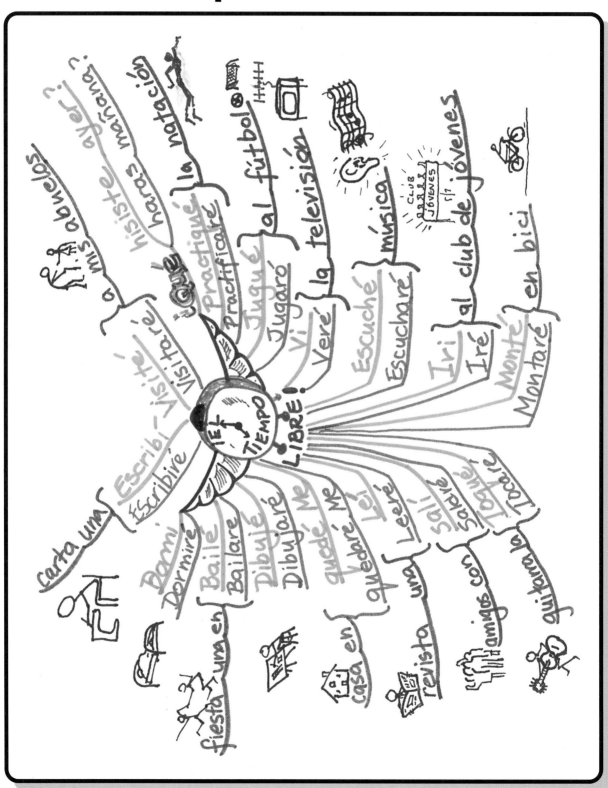

3 En mi tiempo libre

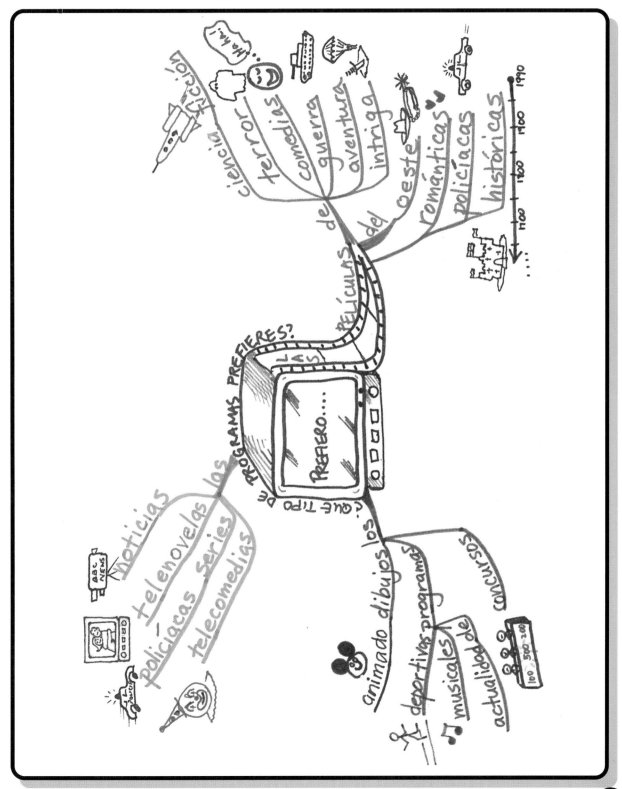

3 En mi tiempo libre

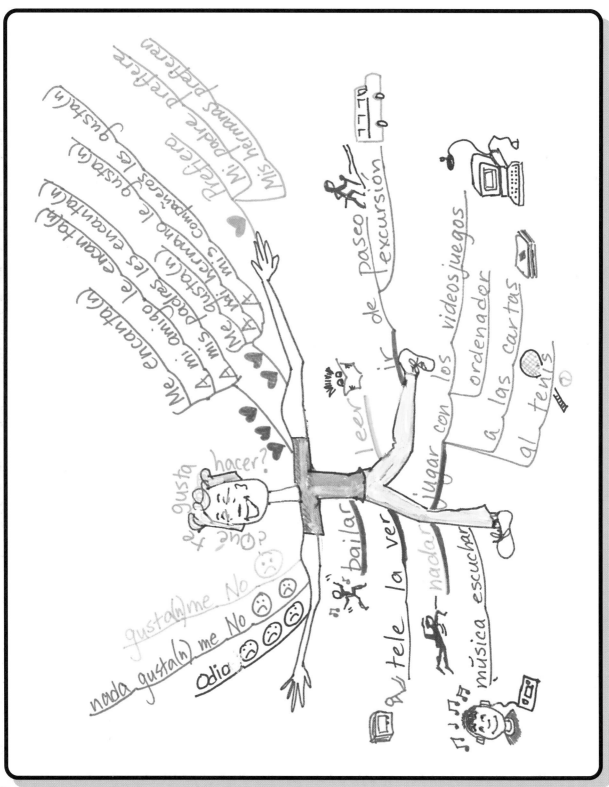

3 En mi tiempo libre

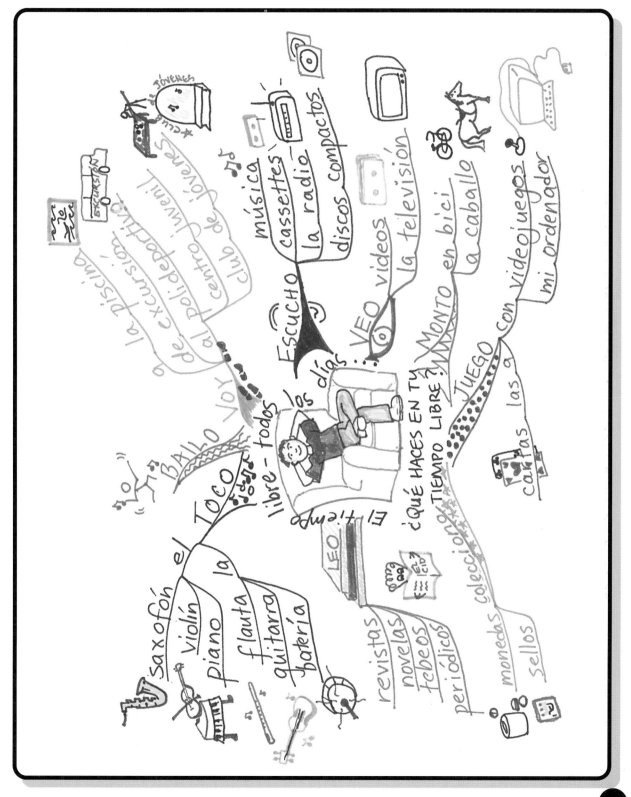

3 En mi tiempo libre

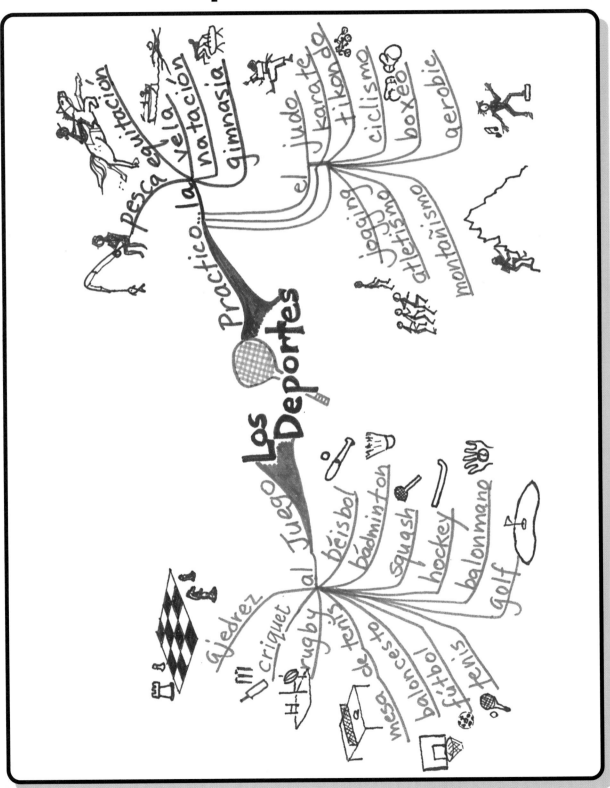

3 En mi tiempo libre

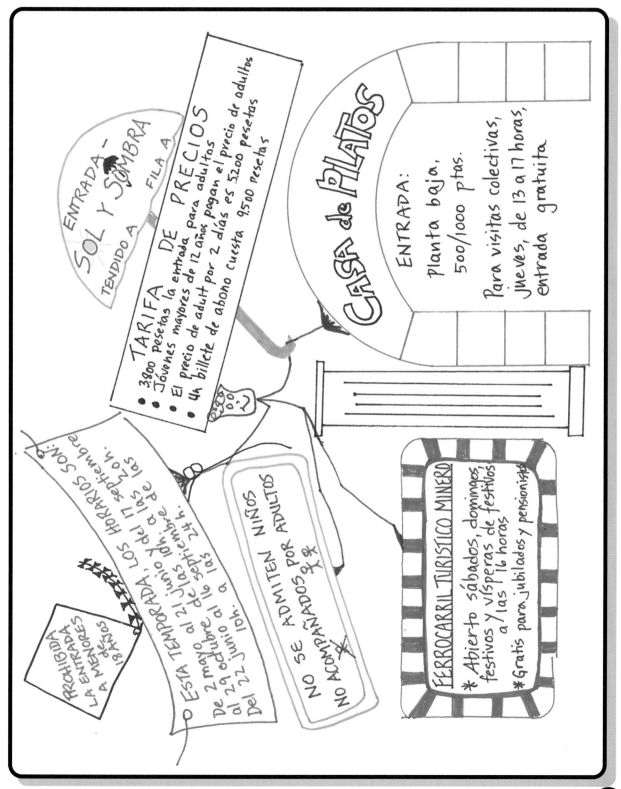

3 En mi tiempo libre

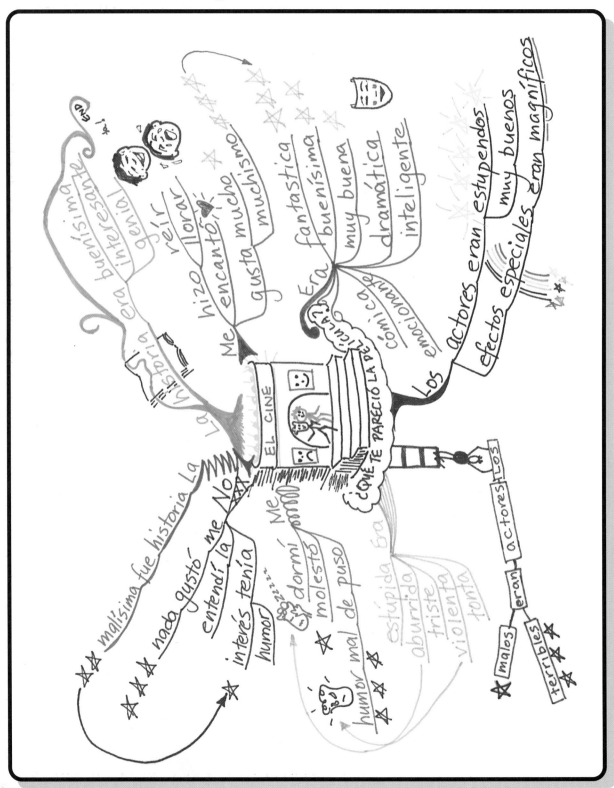

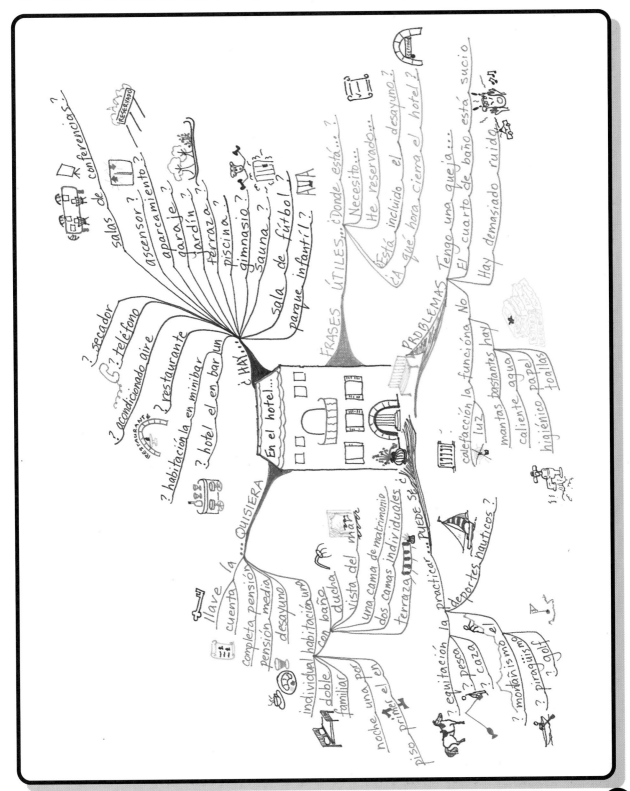

4 De vacaciones

FRASES ÚTILES... ¿Dónde está... ?
Necesito... ?
He reservado... ?
¿Está incluido el desayuno ?
¿A qué hora cierra el hotel ?

PROBLEMAS Tengo una queja...
El cuarto de baño está sucio
Hay demasiado ruido
No calefacción la función
luz
mantas bastantes hay
caliente agua
higiénico papel
toallas

¿ HAY...

salas de conferencias ?
ascensor ?
aparcamiento ?
garaje ?
jardín ?
terraza ?
piscina ?
gimnasio ?
sauna ?
sala de fútbol ?
parque infantil ?

¿ secador
¿ teléfono
¿ acondicionado aire
¿ restaurante
¿ habitación la en minibar
¿ hotel el en bar un

En el hotel...

...QUISIERA
llave la
cuenta
completa pensión
pensión media
desayuno
individual habitación una
doble con baño
ducha
vista del mar
una cama de matrimonio
dos camas individuales
terraza

...PUEDE SE ¿
practicar... la
equitación
¿ pesca
¿ caza
¿ montañismo
¿ piragüismo
¿ golf
deportes náuticos ?

piso primer
noche una por
familiar

4 De vacaciones

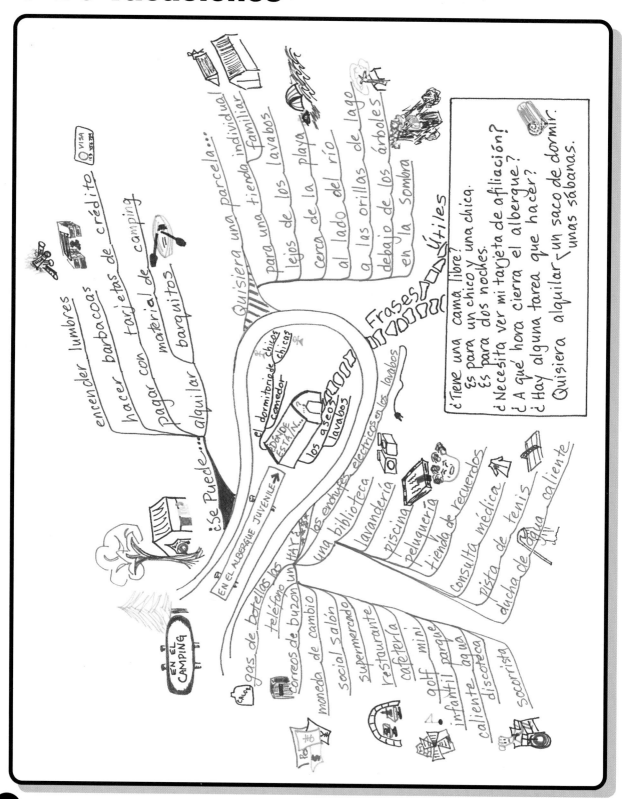

5 Mis vacaciones

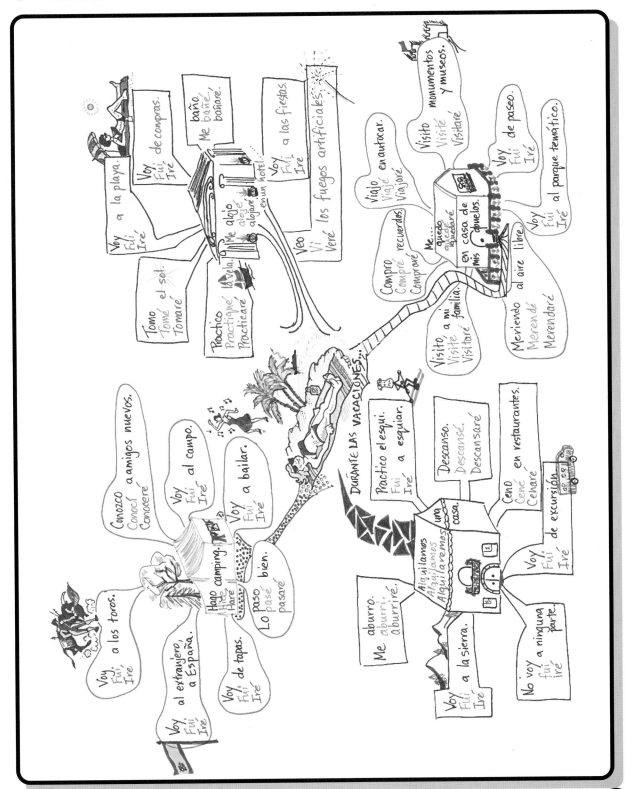

5 Mis vacaciones

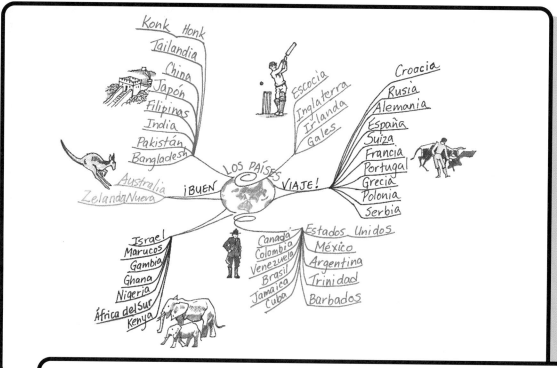

5 Mis vacaciones

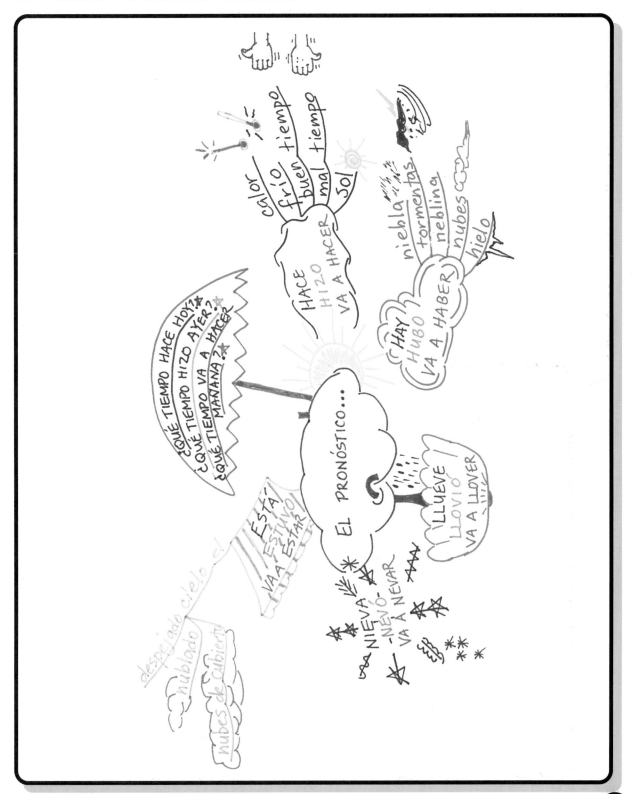

6 Mi pueblo

la ventanilla
la capota
los frenos
neumáticos
el volante
el pasajero
el conductor
el cinturón de seguridad
el motor
el aceite
el agua
batería

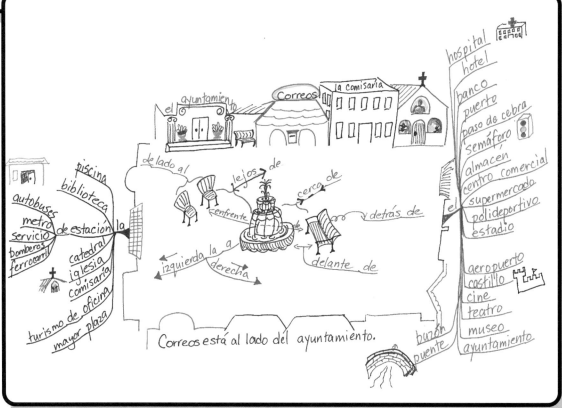

piscina
biblioteca
autobuses
metro
servicio
bomberos
ferrocarril
de estación la
catedral
iglesia
comisaría
turismo de oficina
mayor plaza

el ayuntamiento
Correos
la comisaría

de lado al
lejos de
cerca de
enfrente
y detrás de
izquierda la a
derecha
delante de

hospital
hotel
banco
puerto
paso de cebra
semáforo
almacén
centro comercial
supermercado
el polideportivo
estadio

aeropuerto
castillo
cine
teatro
museo
ayuntamiento

buzón
puente

Correos está al lado del ayuntamiento.

6 Mi pueblo

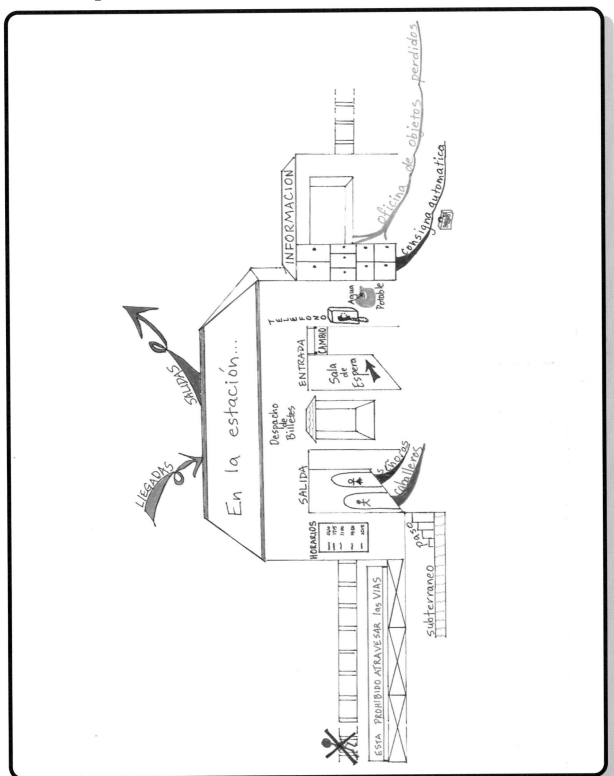

7 De compras

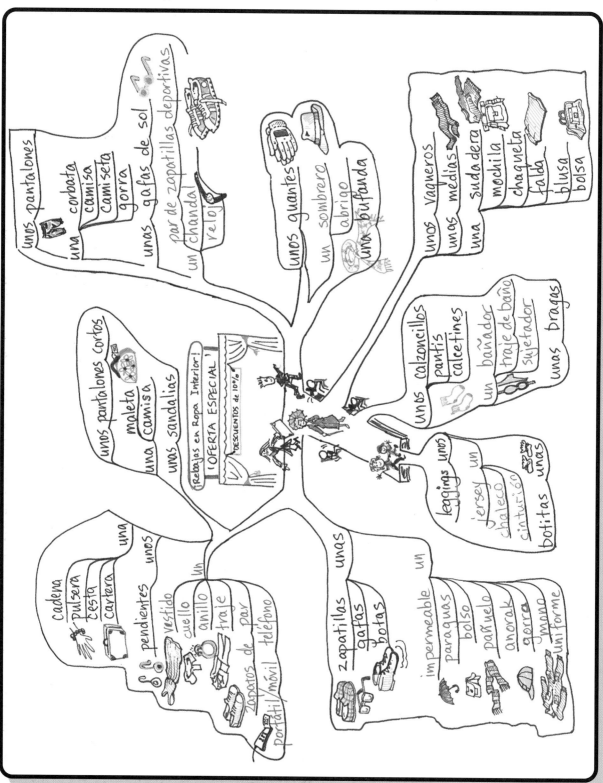

7 De compras

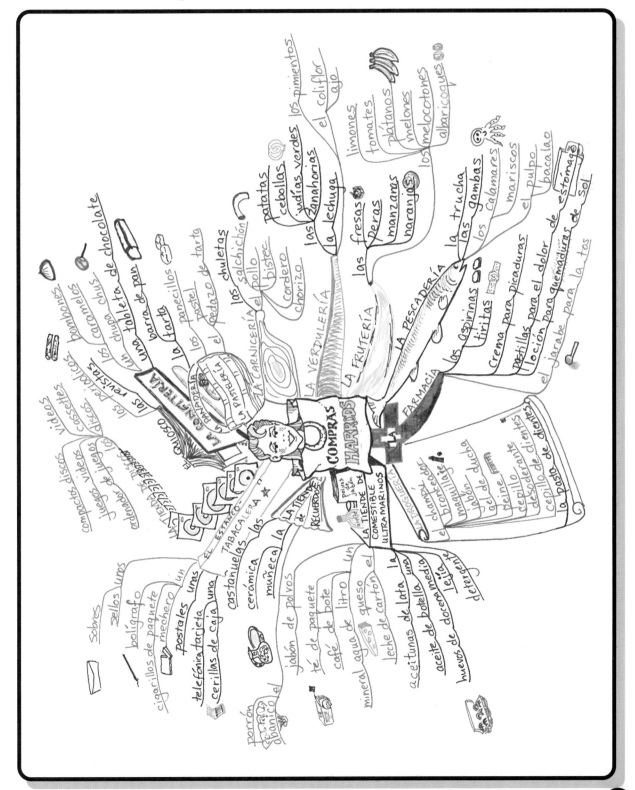

8 En el restaurante

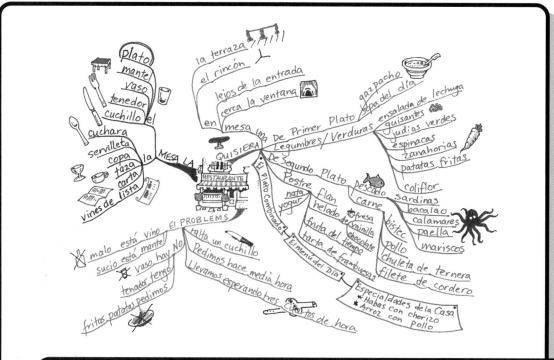

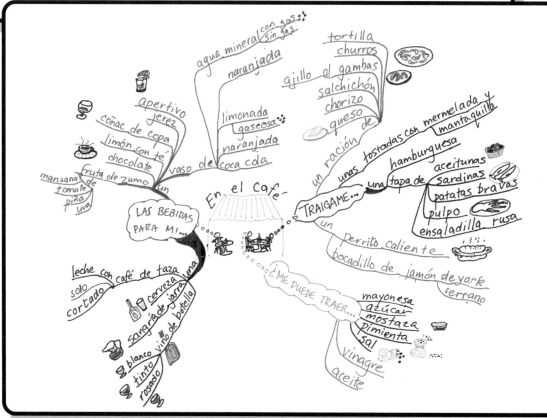

9 En el instituto

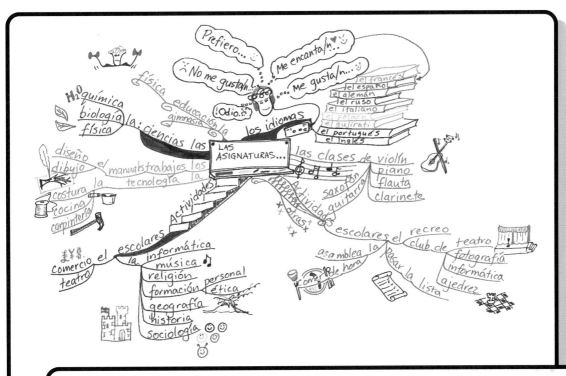

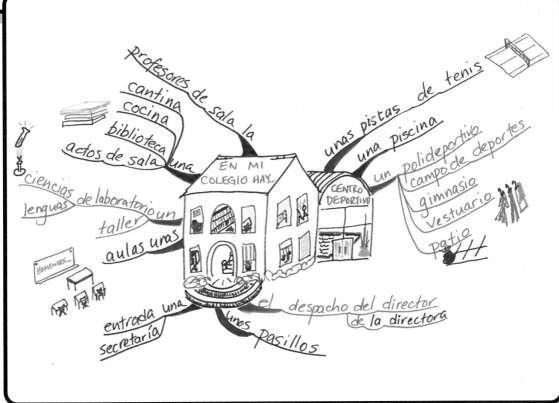

10 En el trabajo

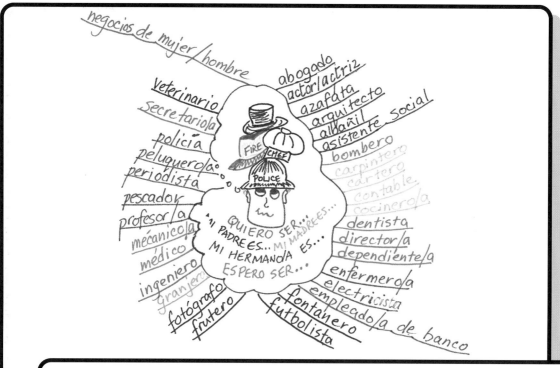

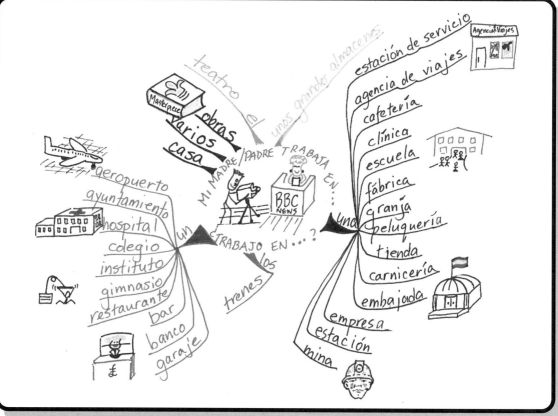

The international world

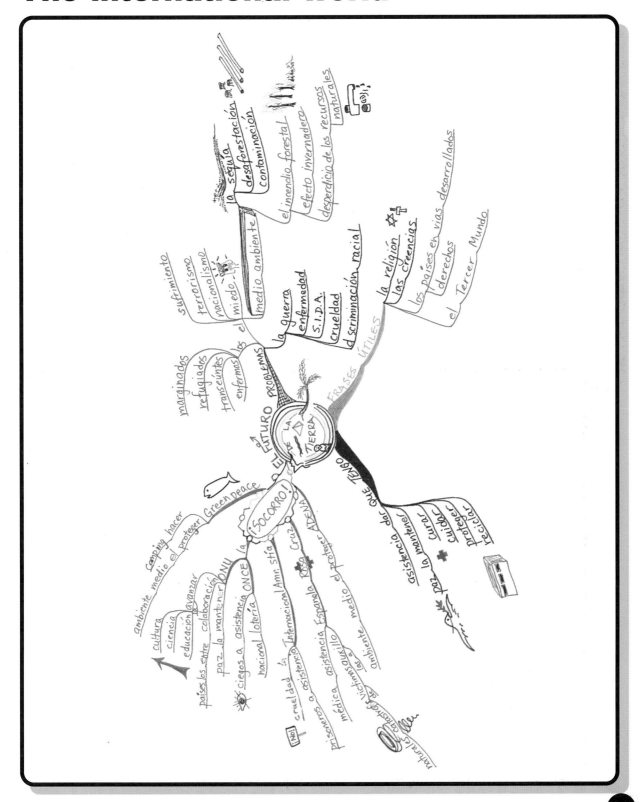

Grammar

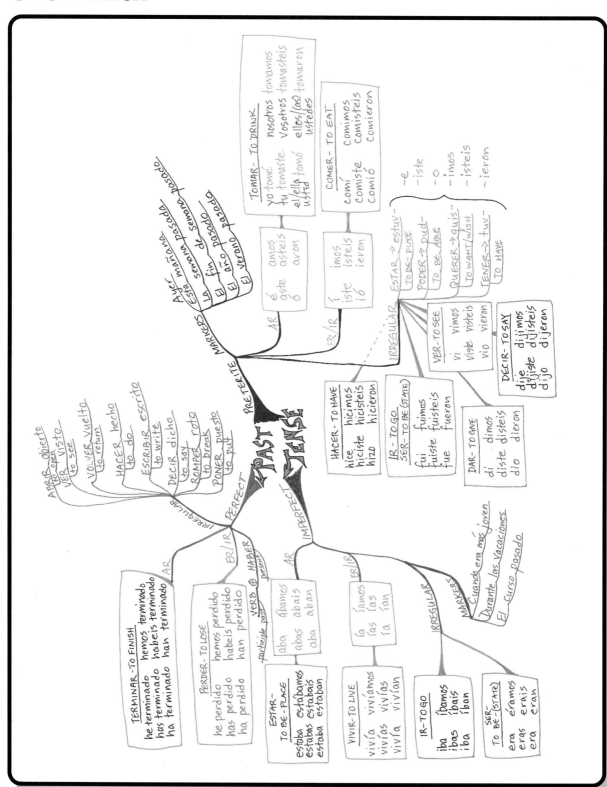

Grammar

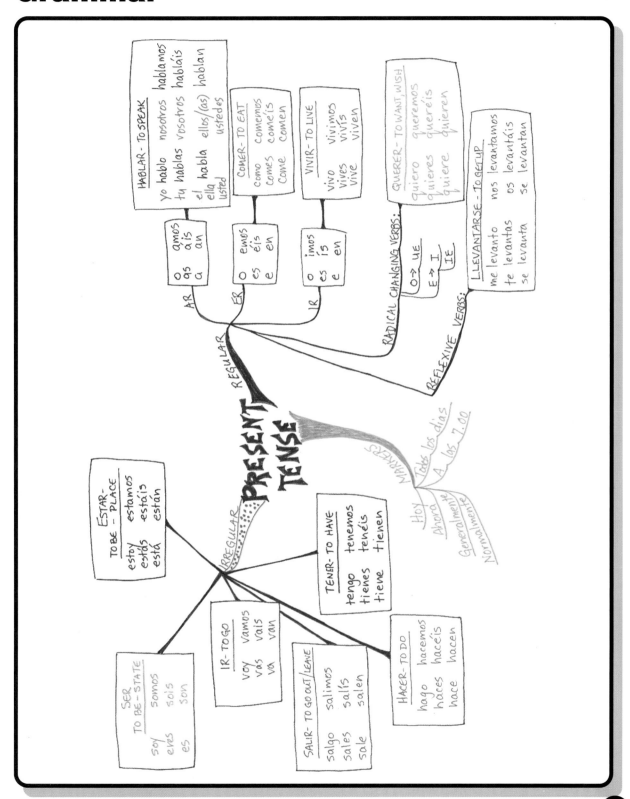

HABLAR - TO SPEAK

yo hablo   nosotros hablamos
tu hablas   vosotros habláis
el habla   ellos/(as) hablan
ella
usted   ustedes

COMER- TO EAT

como   comemos
comes   coméis
come   comen

VIVIR- TO LIVE

vivo   vivimos
vives   vivís
vive   viven

QUERER- TO WANT, WISH

quiero   queremos
quieres   queréis
quiere   quieren

AR
o   amos
as   áis
a   an

ER
o   emos
es   éis
e   en

IR
o   imos
es   ís
e   en

RADICAL CHANGING VERBS:

O → UE
E → I
IE

LLEVANTARSE - TO GET UP

me levanto   nos levantamos
te levantas   os levantáis
se levanta   se levantan

REGULAR

REFLEXIVE VERBS:

PRESENT TENSE

ESTAR - PLACE
TO BE -
estoy   estamos
estás   estáis
está   están

IRREGULAR

TENER- TO HAVE
tengo   tenemos
tienes   tenéis
tiene   tienen

MARKERS:
Hoy   Todos los días
Ahora   A las 7.00
Generalmente
Normalmente

SER
TO BE - STATE
soy   somos
eres   sois
es   son

IR- TO GO
voy   vamos
vas   vais
va   van

SALIR- TO GO OUT/ LEAVE
salgo   salimos
sales   salís
sale   salen

HACER- TO DO
hago   hacemos
haces   hacéis
hace   hacen

Grammar

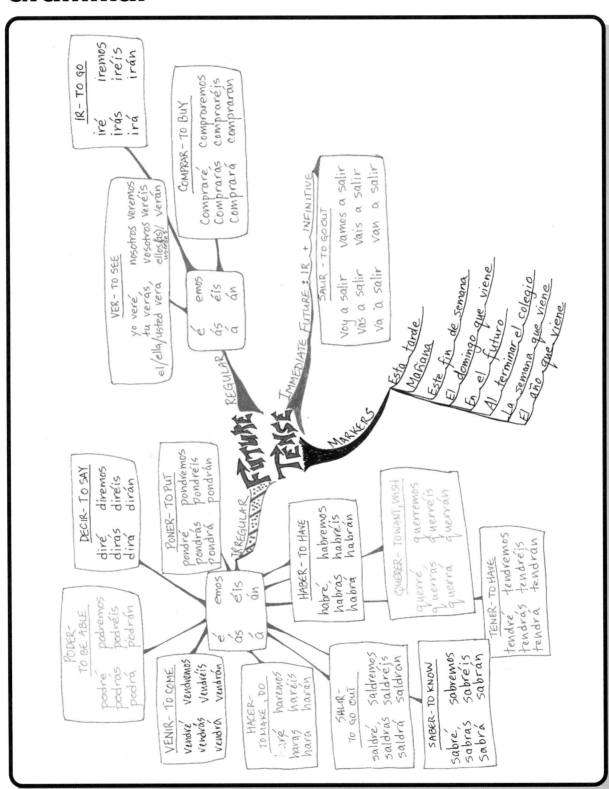

FUTURE TENSE

REGULAR

IR - TO GO
iré   iremos
irás   iréis
irá   irán

COMPRAR - TO BUY
Compraré   Compraremos
Comprarás Compraréis
Comprará   Comprarán

VER - TO SEE
yo veré,   nosotros veremos
tu verás, vosotros veréis
el/ella/usted verá   ellos/as)/ustedes verán

é   emos
ás   éis
á   án

IMMEDIATE FUTURE: IR + INFINITIVE

SALIR - TO GO OUT
Voy a salir   vamos a salir
Vas a salir   vais a salir
va a salir   van a salir

MARKERS

Esta tarde
Mañana
Este fin de semana
El domingo que viene
En el futuro
Al terminar el colegio
La semana que viene
El año que viene

IRREGULAR

DECIR - TO SAY
diré,   diremos
dirás, diréis
dirá   dirán

PONER - TO PUT
pondré   pondremos
pondrás pondréis
pondrá   pondrán

HABER - TO HAVE
habré,   habremos
habrás   habréis
habrá   habrán

QUERER - TO WANT, WISH
querré   querremos
querrás   querréis
querrá   querrán

TENER - TO HAVE
tendré,   tendremos
tendrás, tendréis
tendrá   tendrán

é   emos
ás   éis
á   án

PODER - TO BE ABLE
podré   podremos
podrás   podréis
podrá   podrán

VENIR - TO COME
vendré,   vendremos
vendrás   vendréis
vendrá   vendrán

HACER - TO MAKE, DO
haré   haremos
harás   haréis
hará   harán

SALIR - TO GO OUT
saldré,   saldremos
saldrás   saldréis
saldrá   saldrán

SABER - TO KNOW
sabré,   sabremos
sabrás   sabréis
sabrá   sabrán

Mock exam paper

Before you start

The following mock exam is based on the requirements of a variety of exam boards – all aiming for the same standards. So if you do well in this mock, you should do well in your exam.

The four skills

Listening

Make sure you have a clock, a Spanish-English dictionary, pens and paper to jot ideas on. Have the cassette ready at the start of Side 2. Take five minutes to read the questions – use a dictionary and make notes – before starting the cassette. At the end of the test you will be allowed a further five minutes to check your work, and again refer to a dictionary – do not refer to the dictionary during the test itself. Answer all the questions in the spaces provided. Write neatly and put down all the information. The marks are shown by each question. Allow yourself 30 minutes if you are doing the Foundation level, or 40 minutes if you are doing the Higher.

Speaking

Use ten minutes' preparation time with a dictionary to prepare your role plays. Allow two minutes for the role plays – extra time is allowed for using the cassette recorder. You should have a blank cassette in another recorder to enable you to record your answers, and therefore mark yourself more accurately. If this is not possible, ask a friend to mark you or mark yourself after each question so that you don't forget what you have said. Remember to give opinions and reasons at every opportunity. Make sure you can show that you know how to use the past and future tenses as well as present. In the Conversation section (not included in this mock exam practice) of the Speaking paper try to sound as spontaneous as possible. If you rely on the examiner to prompt you with questions you might get asked a question you don't understand! Let the conversation flow, don't just answer the questions – add comments and detail.

Reading

Don't spend too much time on each question – you might run out of time for other questions. You can always go back to a question when you've done the rest of the paper. Allow yourself 30 minutes if you are doing Foundation, and 50 minutes for Higher – remember to answer all the questions and to write neatly! You may use a dictionary at any time.

Writing

Allow yourself 40 minutes for Foundation, and 50 minutes for Higher.

Listening

Para cada pregunta pon una X en la casilla correcta.

Exercise 1 En casa de tu amiga

¿Qué quiere?

A ☐   B ☐   C ☐   D ☐   [1]

Exercise 2

¿Qué deporte prefiere?

A ☐   B ☐   C ☐   D ☐   [1]

Exercise 3

¿Dónde está el jersey?

A ☐   B ☐   C ☐   D ☐   [1]

Exercise 4   En el centro

¿Dónde está la oficina de turismo?

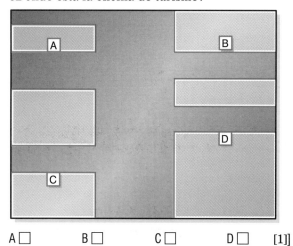

A ☐   B ☐   C ☐   D ☐   [1]]

Exercise 5   En unos grandes almacenes

¿Dónde están las camisetas?

PLANTA BAJA	PRIMERA PLANTA	TERCERA PLANTA	QUINTA PLANTA
A ☐	B ☐	C ☐	D ☐ [1]

Exercise 6   En la estación

¿A qué hora sale el tren?

10.00	12.00	20.00	02.00
A ☐	B ☐	C ☐	D ☐ [1]

Exercise 7   Transportes

¿Cómo va Elena al colegio?

A ☐   B ☐   C ☐   D ☐   [1]

Exercise 8   Planes para mañana

¿Adónde van a ir?

A ☐   B ☐   C ☐   D ☐   [1]

Exercise 9   La familia

Rellena los espacios en esta ficha personal.   [4]

FICHA PERSONAL

Apellidos	Amestoy Fernández		
Nombre(s)	Pilar		
Edad	16		
Nacida el	2 de _____ de 1982		
Hermanos (número)	3		
Nombre(s)	Miguel	**Edad** ____	**Profesión** mecánico
	Enrique	21	_____
	_____	25	enfermera

Exercise 10 El colegio

Rellena los espacios en este horario. [4]

	LUNES	MARTES
Hora		
09.00		Lengua
10.00	Música	Historia
11.00		
11.15	Matemáticas	Geografía
12.15	Dibujo	
1.15	Comida	
3.30	Informática	Literatura
	Lengua	Deportes

Listening

Exercise 11 La visita de Carlos

¿Qué vais a hacer?

A El lunes _____

B El martes _____

C El miércoles _____ [3]

Exercise 12 David Bowie

Completa los detalles.

David Bowie va a visitar Madrid y Barcelona en el mes de _____

Las entradas costarán _____

y puede sacarlas desde _____ [3]

Exercise 13 Vitoria

Your mother mistakenly thinks Vitoria is a person. You explain it is a town in Spain and answer her questions about it.

A In which part of Spain is Vitoria?

_____

B Which is the most important industry?

_____

C What is Vitoria like?

_____

D In which month are the main festivals?

_____ [4]

Listening

Exercise 14 El carácter

Pon una X en la casilla correcta.

1 A ☐ Pablo es una persona ambiciosa.

B ☐ Pablo es una persona que quiere divertirse mucho.

C ☐ Pablo es una persona sensible.

D ☐ Pablo es una persona valiente.

2 A ☐ Inma es una persona ambiciosa.

B ☐ Inma es una persona que quiere divertirse mucho.

C ☐ Inma es una persona sensible.

D ☐ Inma es una persona valiente.

3 A ☐ Carmen es una persona ambiciosa.

B ☐ Carmen es una persona que quiere divertirse mucho.

C ☐ Carmen es una persona sensible.

D ☐ Carmen es una persona valiente.

Exercise 15 Un accidente

Completa los detalles.

Muertos _____

Hora _____

Lugar _____

¿Qué pasó? _____ [4]

Exercise 16 El turismo

Explica lo que es el 'turismo diesel'.

_____ [1]

Exercise 17 En una cafetería

Pon una X en la casilla correcta. [3]

1 ¿De qué se trata esta conversación?

A ☐ El servicio militar

B ☐ La moda

C ☐ El turismo

D ☐ La compra

2 ¿Cómo describirías a Carlos?

A ☐ Valiente

B ☐ Extrovertido

C ☐ Ambicioso

D ☐ Tímido

3 ¿Y a su amigo?

A ☐ Abierto

B ☐ Moderno

C ☐ Tolerante

D ☐ No muy atrevido

Exercise 18 El tiempo

Estás de vacaciones en Motril, en la Costa del Sol. Escuchas los pronósticos del tiempo.

Pon un X en la casilla que corresponde a lo que vas a hacer.

A ☐　　　　B ☐　　　　C ☐　　　[1]

Explica tu decisión:

_____ [2]

Exercise 19 Un empleo

¿Cuáles son las ventajas de este empleo?

_____
_____ [2]

Exercise 20 La vida sana

¿Por qué es sana la vida de esta señora? Escribe dos cosas.

_____
_____ [2]

Exercise 21 Un recado

Te quedas en casa de tu amigo español. Cuando vuelves a casa hay un recado en el contestador automático. ¿Dónde está la discoteca? Escribe tres detalles.

_____
_____
_____ [3]

Exercise 22 Los intereses

Pon una X en la casilla correcta. [3]

1 A ☐ Elena parece una persona seria.

   B ☐ Elena parece una persona ligera.

   C ☐ Elena parece una persona con intereses científicos.

   D ☐ Elena parece una persona con intereses deportivos.

2 A ☐ María parece una persona seria.

   B ☐ María parece una persona ligera.

   C ☐ María parece una persona con intereses científicos.

   D ☐ María parece una persona con intereses deportivos.

3 A ☐ Carlos parece una persona seria.

   B ☐ Carlos parece una persona ligera.

   C ☐ Carlos parece una persona de intereses científicos.

   D ☐ Carlos parece una persona de intereses deportivos.

Exercise 23 Pedro y Maribel

Pon una X en la casilla correcta. [2]

1 ¿Cómo se siente Maribel?

   A ☐ Maribel está enfadada.

   B ☐ Maribel está contenta.

   C ☐ Maribel está cansada.

   D ☐ Maribel está alegre.

2 ¿Cómo son las relaciones entre Pedro y Maribel al fin de la conversación?

   A ☐ divertidas

   B ☐ equivocadas

   C ☐ mejores

   D ☐ peores

Exercise 24 En un restaurante

Pon una X en la casilla correcta. [2]

1 A ☐ La señora es rica.

   B ☐ La señora está loca.

   C ☐ La señora molesta mucho.

   D ☐ La señora olvida mucho.

2 A ☐ El dueño es amable.

   B ☐ El dueño olvida mucho.

   C ☐ El dueño es trabajador.

   D ☐ El dueño se preocupa.

Answers

Listening / Foundation

1 = A	[1]
2 = C	[1]
3 = A	[1]
4 = A	[1]
5 = B	[1]
6 = A	[1]
7 = B	[1]
8 = A	[1]
9 = marzo, 28, estudiante, María	[4]
10 = inglés, recreo, ciencias, 4.30	[4]

TOTAL = [16]

Listening / Foundation + Higher

11 A = restaurante	
B = cine / película	
C = discoteca / bailar	[3]
12 A = setiembre	
B = 6.000 pesetas	
C = esta semana	[3]
13 A = north / Basque Country / near Bilbao	
B = woollen	
C = lively / lots of sports facilities	
D = August	[4]

TOTAL = [10]

Speaking

Role play 1

En la tienda de comestibles.

You are in a food shop and need to buy two items. The part of the shopkeeper is on the cassette. Remember to greet the shopkeeper and to end the conversation politely.

[10]

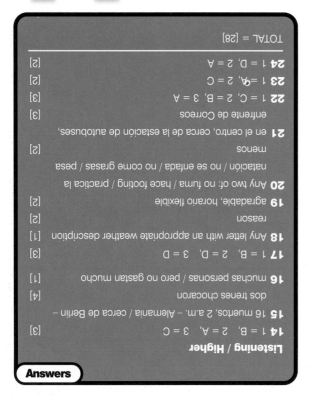

Role play 2

You are in Valencia station. The part of the ticket office clerk is recorded on the cassette. The clerk opens the conversation.

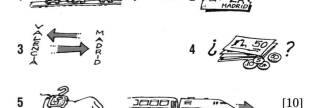

[10]

Speaking

Role play 3

Your English friend who speaks only English falls ill while you are together in Spain. You will hear the doctor's part on the cassette, and the doctor starts the conversation.

1 Explica por qué habéis venido a la consulta y por qué tu amigo/a no le habla.

2 Dile dos síntomas que tiene tu amigo/a.

3 Contesta la pregunta.

4 Di en qué hotel estáis y dónde está.

5 Cuando receta unas pastillas, haz una pregunta sobre el tratamiento. [20]

Speaking

Role play 4

You have seen this advertisement for summer jobs at the Camping Vistamar and you decide to ring up to find out more information and to give details about yourself. You will hear the employee on the cassette, and the employee begins the conversation.

CAMPING VISTAMAR
Temporada de verano de 1998
Necesitamos
camareros/camareras
dependientes/dependientas
chicos/chicas para guardería niños
Tfo. 72 33 44

● ¿Razón de la llamada?
● Detalles personales
● Horas de trabajo [20]

Answers

Speaking / Foundation

Mark each sentence using the following scale:

0 If what you say is inappropriate and does not communicate the information.
1 If what you say is appropriate even if it is not accurate, or if part of the information is missing.
2 If what you say is correct and appropriate, even if there are minor mistakes.

1

Tape Buenos días.
You Buenos días.
Tape ¿En qué puedo servirle?
You Quisiera una botella de Coca Cola, un paquete de patatas fritas, un paquete de galletas. (any appropriate amount of the following, e.g. 200 gramos de .... medio kilo de .... un pedazo de ...) queso, pescado, y chorizo / salchicha / salchichón. (any two)
Tape Tenga.
You ¿Cuánto es?
Tape Son mil quinientas pesetas.
You Gracias.
Tape De nada.
You Adiós.
Tape Adiós.

Total = [10]

2

Tape Buenos días, ¿qué desea?
You Quisiera un billete par Madrid.
Tape Sí. ¿De qué clase quiere?
You De segunda clase.
Tape Muy bien. ¿Billete sencillo?

Answers

You No, un billete de ida y vuelta.
Tape Vale.
You ¿Cuánto es?
Tape Son 4300 pesetas.
You ¿A qué hora sale el tren?
Tape Sale a las diez.

Total = [10]

Speaking / Higher

Role plays 3 and 4

Mark each sentence using the following scale:

0 If what you say is inappropriate and does not communicate the information.
1 If what you say is appropriate even if it is not accurate, or part of the information is missing.
2 If what you say is correct and appropriate, even if there are minor mistakes.
3 If what you say is complete, not ambiguous and without any persistent mistakes such as wrong use of tense, persons, pronouns, etc. which might cause difficulty in communication.
4 If what you say is correct + appropriate (no mistakes).

3

Tape Buenos días. ¿Qué pasa?
You Mi amigo/a está enfermo/a / no se siente bien.
Tape Bueno, y ¿qué le pasa?
You (Choose any two symptoms. Remember: use the correct person i.e. not Me duele ... not Le duele ... and Tiene ... not Tengo...)
Tape Y, ¿cuándo empezó esto?
You Choose a day (or yesterday).
Tape Vale. Y ¿dónde estáis alojados/as?
You Nos estamos alojando / quedando en el hotel. (any name will do) En la plaza mayor (or any location)
Tape Buen, pues, le voy a recetar unas pastillas.
You ¿Cuántas veces al día hay que tomarlas? (you are required to ask about dosage or something similarly appropriate)

Total = [20]

4

Tape Camping Vistamar. Dígame.
You Estoy llamando para / Quiero pedir información sobre empleos en el camping. (you can ask about a specific job e.g. Quiero más información sobre los puestos de niñero/a)

Answers

4 (continued)

Tape ¿Puede darme unos detalles personales?

You Me llamo …. tengo … años … hablo español e inglés, soy estudiante. (choose any relevant personal details)

Tape ¿Qué experiencia tiene de este tipo de trabajo?

You Hago de (remember you don't have to tell the truth) canguro. / He trabajado como dependient en unos grandes almacenes. / Trabajé de cajere en un supermercado el verano pasado.

Tape ¿Cuándo puede comenzar?

You Puedo empezar el primero de junio.

Tape ¿Tiene alguna pregunta?

You ¿Cuáles son las horas laborales?

Tape De 8h a 12h y de 15h a 19h de lunes a viernes.

Total = [20]

Reading F

Exercise 1   El camping

En una tienda de artículos de camping.

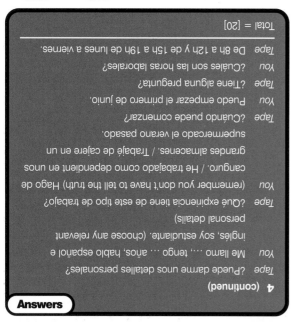

8,900
595
660
890
3,195
995

¿Cuánto cuesta, …

ejemplo

   … una tienda de campaña?   8.900 pesetas

A … un saco de dormir? _____

B … una toalla? _____

C … unas gafas de sol? _____

[3]

Exercise 2

Direcciones para el camping.

> **Sube la calle San Fermín.**
> **Coge la segunda a la derecha.**
> **El camping está a la izquierda, al lado de Correos.**

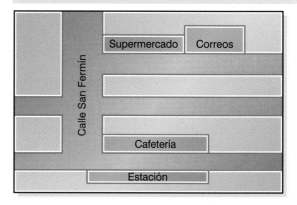

Calle San Fermín

Supermercado | Correos

Cafetería

Estación

Marca con una X el camping en este plan.   [1]

Exercise 3

A C T I V I D A D E S

Sábado	
9:00	Jugar al fútbol
10:00	Pescar
11:00	Patinar sobre hielo
12:00	Montar en bicicleta
2:00	Jugar al baloncesto
3:00	Natación
4:00	Jugar al tenis
5:00	Montar a caballo

A   B   C   D

¿A qué hora puedes hacer estas actividades?

_____ [4]

Exercise 4 — En el supermercado

Pon una X en la casilla correcta.

1 ¿Qué compras para ducharte?

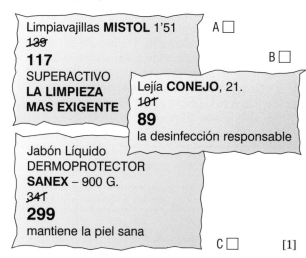

Limpiavajillas **MISTOL** 1'51
~~139~~
117
SUPERACTIVO
LA LIMPIEZA MAS EXIGENTE

A ☐

Lejía **CONEJO**, 21.
~~101~~
89
la desinfección responsable

B ☐

Jabón Líquido
DERMOPROTECTOR
SANEX – 900 G.
~~341~~
299
mantiene la piel sana

C ☐ [1]

2 ¿En qué sección del supermercado está la naranjada?

DROGUERIA	ULTRAMARINOS	BEBIDAS
A ☐	B ☐	C ☐ [1]

3 ¿Cuál de estos productos compra un vegetariano?

16 croquetas 'MAHESO' CARNE	16 croquetas 'MAHESO' QUESO	16 croquetas 'MAHESO' POLLO	16 croquetas 'MAHESO' JAMON
A ☐	B ☐	C ☐	D ☐ [1]

4 Aquí hay una lista de observaciones sobre este producto.

LECHE PASCUAL Uperisada

Especial para ti ¡Mira, mira!

Te llena de energía y de regalos.

Hemos pensado la manera de ponerte la **LECHE PASCUAL** más cómoda y se nos ha ocurrido la MINI, especial para ti.

Puedes llevártela en la cartera al 'cole' para reponer energía en el recreo. Puedes sacarla contigo de excursión y llevártela de merienda, con el 'bocata'.

Tiene todas las proteínas, vitaminas y minerales que necesitas para la vida tan dura que llevas.

¡Y, además, está buenísima!

	Verdad	Mentira	No se sabe
Ejemplo El paquete es pequeño.	✗		
A Leche Pascual es buena para la salud.			
B Es barata.			
C Es ideal para los picnics.			

5 ¿Cuáles son los premios del concurso?

ADIVINE EL PESO DE ESTA BOLSA Y GANE 10.000.000 PTAS. Y 1.000 PREMIOS MAS

L A   B U E N A   C O M P R A

Además de estar comprando la mejor calidad al mejor precio, ahora le ofrecemos una promoción de peso.

Haga su buena compra de todos los días. Ahora, usted puede llegar a ganar ¡10.000.000 de pesetas y uno de los mil Udakitos, el muñeco que encantará a sus hijos!

A _____

B _____ [2]

Reading

Exercise 5 — Un anuncio para la radio 'SER'

Escoge la frase correcta para cada dibujo. Pon un número en la casilla.

LAS MEJORES FORMAS DE PONER SER.

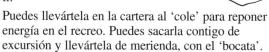

Ejemplo ③   A ☐   B ☐   C ☐ [3]

La SER encima	1	7 de julio San SERmín	4
La SER a todo tren	2	La SER en el bolsillo	5
La SER con los ojos cerrados	3	La SER por deporte	6

Exercise 6 Quieres revelar unas fotos

**N° 1 EN PRECIO
JORDI BAS
FOTO NO CERRAMOS AL MEDIODIA**

La tienda está abierta –

Pon una X en la casilla correcta.   [1]

A ☐	A medianoche
B ☐	Sólo por la tarde
C ☐	Sólo por la mañana
D ☐	Todo el día

Reading

Exercise 7 En la estación de servicio

You are on holiday in Spain with your parents who don't speak Spanish – so you help them out at the petrol station.

**MAS DE 5.000 TITULARES SERVIRED
VAN A GANAR MILES DE LITROS DE GASOLINA.**

Entre el 1 de Junio y el 31 de Agosto, cada vez que pague la gasolina con su Tarjeta ServiRed prodrá recuperar, el importe de la operación realizada, si ésta resulta premiada. Y lo que es mejor, puede conseguir gratis, además, la gasolina de todo el aña. Un año sin pagar la gasolina es el regalo de su Tarjeta ServiRed.

Su Tarjeta Visa Electron en Hipermercados, Grandes Almacenes, Restaurantes y en dos millones y medio de establecimientos más. 🔅 *ServiRed*

Su Tarjeta VISA Electron

Why would it be a good idea to pay for petrol with a SeriRed credit card?

_____   [1]

Exercise 8 En la sección de jugetes

BUSY ELEPHANT
(Elefante de actividades)
6 meses a 2 años
Bebé elefante con seis divertidos juegos. Puede adaptarse a la cuna o al parque. Es blandito y de tacto suave. Guarda un ratón en el bolsillo. La oreja derecha cruje y la izquierda es un sonajero. En la trompa mantiene una pelota en equilibrio. Las patas llevan un espejo y un dial de teléfono.
Se puede lavar a máquina.

1 Pon una X en la casilla correcta.   [3]

	Verdad	Mentira	No se sabe
Ejemplo Es bueno para un bebé de 24 meses.	X		
A Tiene dos sonidos diferentes.			
B Las patas llevan cuatro actividades diferentes.			
C Se puede lavar en la lavadora.			

2 ¿Qué partes del cuerpo puedes cambiar? Indica cuatro.

LA FAMILIA POTATO

2 – 6 años
El señor Potato, la señora Potato y el bebé Potato componen esta divertida familia. Con 33 accesorios para combinar y caracterizar de muchas formas a estos personajes. Los accesorios se guardan en el compartimento situado en la espalda de los Potatos.

Ojos, bocas, pendientes, zapatos, sombreros, orejas, narices, bigotes se insertan en patatas de plástico.

_____

_____

_____   [4]

Exercise 9 — Consejos de 'Acción Cívica'

¿Qué problema intenta resolver la 'Acción Cívica'?

CONSEJOS de ACCION CIVICA	CONSEJOS de ACCION CIVICA
Utiliza las papeleras	No ensucies

_____ [1]

Exercise 10 — Jorge Valdano

JORGE VALDANO

Ganar con buenas maneras

El entrenador del Real Madrid ha empezado la Liga con triunfos.

Bajo su trato exquisito, se esconde un luchador feroz, un ganador nato. Jorge Valdano nació en Argentina hace 38 años y vino a España con 20 para jugar en el Alavés. Allí triunfó, conoció a una chica y se enamoró, pero le costó tres años llevarla al altar porque ella no le hacía ni caso. Luego pasó al Zaragoza y al Real Madrid, fue campeón del Mundo con Argentina y una hepatitis le hizo colgar las botas a los 31 años. Sin dejarse abatir, se hizo entrenador, y sus éxitos en el Tenerife le han abierto el camino.

Aquí hay una lista de las etapas de la vida de Jorge Valdano. Indica con los números de 1 a 7 el órden correcto de las etapas. [4]

1	Se casó a los 23 años	
2	Cuando tenía 20 años vino a España	1
3	Jugó en el equipo del Real Madrid	
4	A los 31 años dejó de jugar al fútbol	
5	Jugó en el equipo del Alavés	
6	Jugó en el equipo del Zaragoza	4
7	Se hizo entrenador del Real Madrid	7

Exercise 11 — Carta de Cristina Martínez

Lees esta carta de Cristina Martínez.

CANARIAS: DEL AVION AL CAMELLO

Era la primera vez que subía a un avión. ¡Qué divertido! A la llegada hubo un lío de maletas, una por aquí, otra por allá, que ésa es la mía, que es la tuya … Al final cogimos las nuestras y nos fuimos al hotel.

¡Oh, sorpresa! En vez de una cama, en mi cuarto habían puesto una cuna. Ellos creían que yo era un bebé, pero por fin todo se solucionó.

Los días transcurrieron entre viajes conociendo la isla de Tenerife, baños en la piscina, compras y paseos. Uno de esos viajes, a Lanzarote, fue el más divertido. Empezó y terminó en un avión que se descuajeringaba por todas partes, dando botes y con gente mareada delante y detrás del avión. Y mi hermana y yo pidiendo más botes porque parecía una 'montaña rusa'.

A lomos de un camello

En la visita turística nos montamos en camellos. ¡Jo, qué miedo pasé!

Estuvimos en un sitio que se llama Los Jameos del Agua, que era precioso. Y en el Teide, las piscinas de lava de Garachico, el Drago milenario, los platanares, el Loro Park, las piscinas Martínez y el Acantilado de los Gigantes. Hicimos un viaje por la isla, en el que mi padre, como es custumbre en él, se perdió y nos llevó por una carretera infernal. Todo fue estupendo.

Cristina Martínez

1 ¿Cómo se sintió Cristina …?

A ¿En el vuelo a Canarias?

_____

B ¿Al entrar en la habitación de su hotel?

_____

C ¿Montada en camello?

_____

2 ¿Qué le suele pasar a su padre?

_____ [4]

Exercise 12 Lees este artículo

CADA PAIS EUROPEO CASTIGA CON PENAS DISTINTAS A LOS 'NARCOS'

Un narcotraficante detenido en Bélgica es castigado con cinco años de prisión. Si es arrestado en Alemania, la pena será de 15 años. Pero si ha cometido el delito en el Reino Unido, la condena será de cadena perpetua. Un drogodependiente no podrá curarse en centros de El Patriarca en Bélgica, porque allí fueron cerrados por 'falta de higiene' y 'malos tratos'. Pero sí podrá hacerlo en España, donde esta asociación funciona regularmente, con excepción de Cataluña. A partir de ejemplos de este tipo se ha planteado en Bruselas un debate sobre la necesidad de contar con un convenio común europeo sobre la droga.

1 Rellena la tabla con la información correcta según el artículo. [3]

PAIS	SENTENCIA
A Bélgica	_____
B Alemania	_____
C Reino Unido	_____

2 ¿Por qué se cerraron los centros de El Patriarca en Bélgica?

_____ [2]

3 ¿En qué parte de España no se puede curarse en los centros?

_____ [1]

Answers

Reading / Foundation

1 A = 8.900;   B = 660;   D = 595 [3]
2 X next to Correos on the map [1]
3 A = 11:00;   B = 9:00;   C = 3:00;   D = 5:00 [4]
4 1 = C;   2 = C;   3 = B [3]
4 A = Verdad;   B = No se sabe;   C = Verdad [3]
5 A = 10.000.000 pts.;   B = Udakitos or muñeco [5]

TOTAL = [19]

Reading / Foundation + Higher

5 A = 5;   B = 6;   C = 2 [3]

---

6 = D [1]

7 You are given a whole year's petrol as a gift. [1]

Reading / Higher
8 1 A = Verdad   B = Mentira   C = Verdad [3]
2 Any 4 of: ojos / bocas / orejas / narices / bigotes [1]
9 La suciedad or la basura [1]
10 3, 1, 5, 6, 2, 4, 7
11 1 A = Emocionada
  B = Sorprendida
  C = Asustada/tenía miedo [4]
2 Perderse
12 1 A = 5 años de prisión
  B = 15 años de prisión
  C = Cadena perpetua [3]
2 Falta de higiene, Malos tratos
3 Cataluña [3]

TOTAL = [16]

Answers

Writing

Exercise 1

Rellena el formulario con tu información personal.

NACIONALIDAD	
ANIMALES EN CASA	
ASIGNATURA PREFERIDA EN EL COLEGIO	
COLOR DE OJOS	
DEPORTE PREFERIDO	
PASATIEMPO FAVORITO	
OTROS PASATIEMPOS	
COMIDA QUE NO TE GUSTA	
COMIDA QUE TE GUSTA	
BEBIDA QUE TE GUSTA	

[10]

Exercise 2

Tu amigo español llegó a tu casa ayer. Esta mañana, tú tienes que salir, pero ¡tu amigo está todavía en la cama! Le escribes un mensaje. Escribe unas 25 palabras, e incluye la información siguiente:

¿Dónde?   Tú

¿A qué hora?

Desayuno   ¿qué?   ¿dónde?

Sugerencias para la mañana   ¿Qué programa?

Writing

Exercise 3

Recibes esta carta de tu amiga española. Escríbele una carta contestando sus preguntas (aproximadamente 70 palabras).

¡Hola!   Zaragoza, 19 de junio

Gracias por tu carta. Las clases terminaron la semana pasada y el sábado tuvimos una fiesta. ¿Y tú? ¿Qué hiciste el fin de semana?

Creo que voy a pasar las próximas cuatro semanas en casa de mis primos. Luego voy a trabajar en una tienda de ropa.

¿Y tú? ¿Cuándo te tomas las vacaciones? ¿Qué planes tienes?

Escribe pronto,

Un abrazo,

Maite

Writing

Exercise 4

El colegio de idiomas 'Shakespeare' quiere atraer a los estudiantes españoles a aprender el inglés aquí en Gran Bretaña. Escribe el texto de un folleto para el colegio 'Shakespeare' de tu región.

Hay unas notas para ayudarte:

'Shakespeare' – buen colegio ¿por qué?

¿Ventajas de estudiar en Gran Bretaña?

Mejor estación del año para visitar, ¿por qué?

¿Cómo llegar desde España?

Alojamiento en familia, ¿buena idea? ¿por qué?

Y, ¿en el tiempo libre?

¿Qué ofrece la región para los españoles?

Writing / Foundation + Higher

Exercise 3

Mark yourself according to content, use of language and accuracy. You can give yourself up to six marks for each of the criteria making a total of 18. Use the following three scales.

Content

0   Hardly any relevant information communicated to a native speaker of Spanish.

1–2   Between ⅓ and ½ of the tasks are covered, with the minimum message communicated in each one. The response is basic and there may be some points missing.

3–4   Between ½ and ⅔ of the tasks are covered, with the minimum message communicated in each. In several of the tasks covered, the response is more than minimal.

5–6   All, or more than ⅔ of the tasks are covered, and the minimum message is communicated in each one. In many of the tasks there is evidence of ability to go beyond the minimal level of response.

Use of language

0   The language used is too limited to merit a mark.

1–2   Between ⅓ and ½ of the messages are communicated in a simple but intelligible way. The language used may not be fully appropriate to the tasks, and the word order and structure may not be confident.

3–4   Between ½ and ⅔ of the messages are communicated using appropriate language.

5–6   All or more than ⅔ of the messages are communicated. The language is effective and appropriate. Where necessary, use is made of past, present and future tenses.

Accuracy

0   Mistakes prevent communication.

1–2   Between ⅓ and ½ of the messages are intelligible, despite mistakes which could lead to misunderstanding by a native speaker of Spanish.

3–4   Between ½ and ⅔ of the messages are communicated. Although there may be some mistakes and some items left out, the messages are not difficult for a native speaker of Spanish to understand.

5–6   All or more than ⅔ of the messages are communicated accurately enough for a native speaker to understand. There are only minor mistakes and occasional items left out.

Writing / Higher

Exercises 4 and 5

Mark yourself according to content, use of language and accuracy. You can give yourself up to eight marks for each of the criteria, making a total of 24. Use the following three scales.

Content

0   Little relevant information communicated to the native speaker.

1–2   Ability to respond to all or more than ⅔ of the set tasks. The level of response is minimal.

3–4   Ability to extract and communicate information in all or ⅔ of the set tasks. Although self-expression is limited, there is evidence of ability to go beyond the minimal level of response in several of the tasks.

5–6   Ability to respond reasonably fully to all or ⅔ of the set tasks. Can demonstrate some ability to describe, give personal accounts and give opinions.

7–8   Ability to respond fully to all the tasks even though minor points may be left out. There is little difficulty in self-expression. Ability to elaborate on points, to give full descriptions and to effectively communicate attitudes and opinions.

Use of language

0   The language used is too weak to merit a mark.

1–2   Although the language is not wide in scope, it is appropriate and enough to communicate the messages.

3–4   The language used is appropriate and goes beyond the minimal response. The writing has some coherence and continuity. Where necessary, past, present and future tenses are used.

5–6   The language used is coherent even though communication may be disjointed in places. There is variety of expression used in descriptions, accounts and opinions.

7–8   The language used is appropriate and effective. The writing is coherent and continuous. Descriptions and accounts are full and opinions clearly communicated.

Accuracy

0   Mistakes prevent communication.

1–2   The set tasks are communicated without mistakes in grammar and vocabulary leading to misunderstanding. Some effort by the reader may be required.

3–4   Although mistakes might interfere with immediate comprehension, the set tasks can be understood without difficulty.

5–6   Mistakes are minor and do not affect communication.

7–8   There are very few mistakes in grammar or vocabulary. Where there are mistakes, they may occur from complicated structures being used to elaborate on given points.

12

Grammar

VERBS

1 Formation: Regular Verbs

There are three verb endings for regular verbs: **ar**, **er**, **ir**. They all follow the same pattern:

HABLAR = to speak
present

habl**o**	I speak
habl**as**	you speak
habl**a**	he / she / it speaks, you (polite) speak
habl**amos**	we speak
habl**áis**	you (plural) speak
habl**an**	they speak, you (polite plural) speak

preterite

habl**é**	I spoke
habl**aste**	you spoke
habl**ó**	he / she / it spoke, you (polite) spoke
habl**amos**	we spoke
habl**asteis**	you spoke (plural)
habl**aron**	they spoke, you (polite plural) spoke

COMER = to eat
present

com**o**	I eat
com**es**	you speak
com**e**	he / she / it eats, you (polite) eat
com**emos**	we eat
com**éis**	you (plural) eat
com**en**	they eat, you (polite plural) eat

preterite

com**í**	I ate
com**iste**	you ate

com**ió**	he / she / it ate, you (polite) ate
com**imos**	we ate
com**isteis**	you ate (plural)
com**ieron**	they ate you (polite plural) ate

VIVIR = to live
present

viv**o**	I live
viv**es**	you live
viv**e**	he / she / it lives, you (polite) live
viv**imos**	we live
viv**ís**	you live (plural)
viv**en**	they live, you (polite plural) live

preterite

viv**í**	I lived
viv**iste**	you lived
viv**ió**	he / she / it lived you (polite) lived
viv**imos**	we lived
viv**isteis**	you lived (plural)
viv**ieron**	they lived, you (polite plural) lived

The familiar form

You use the second person of the verb when you are talking to friends, relatives and children. If you are talking to one person in this familiar form you use the **tú** form:
¿Hablas inglés?
¿Qué comes para el desayuno?

If you are talking to more than one person in the familiar form you use the second person plural:
Habláis español muy bien.
¿A qué hora coméis?

The polite form

When you are talking to an adult who is not a close friend or relative you use the polite form, **usted** or **ustedes** (abbreviated to **Ud** or **Vd**, **Uds** or **Vds**):
¿Cómo se llama Ud?
Tome usted.
Perdonen Uds.

'-ar' verbs

Verbs which have the '-**ar**' endings in the infinitive and follow the pattern of endings above, are:

infinitive	*present*	*preterite*
arreglar = to tidy	arregl**o**	arregl**é**
ayudar = to help	ayud**o**	ayud**é**
escuchar = to help	escuch**o**	escuch**é**
lavar = to wash	lav**o**	lav**é**
limpiar = to clean	limpi**o**	limpi**é**
mirar = to watch, to look (at)	mir**o**	mir**é**
pasar = to pass (by), happen, spend (time)	pas**o**	pas**é**
tomar = to take	tom**o**	tom**é**
hablar = to speak	habl**o**	habl**é**
llevar = to take (away), to wear	llev**o**	llev**é**

Llegar and sacar are similar, but they have spelling changes in the first person singular of the preterite:

sacar = to take out / get	sac**o**	sa**qué**
llegar = to arrive	lleg**o**	lle**gué**

'-er' verbs

Verbs which have '-**er**' endings in the infinitive and which follow the pattern above, are:

BEBER = to drink

present	*preterite*
bebo	bebí

VER = to see

present	*preterite*
veo	vi

'-ir' verbs

Here is a verb which has an '-**ir**' ending in the infinitive and which follows the pattern above:

ESCRIBIR = to write

present	*preterite*
escribo	escribí

2 Formation: Irregular verbs

Some verbs do not follow the regular pattern. They are called irregular verbs.

CONOCER = to know (someone)		ESTAR = to be	
present	*preterite*	*present*	*preterite*
conozco	conocí	estoy	estuve
conoces	conociste	estás	estuviste
conoce	conoció	está	estuvo
conocemos	conocimos	estamos	estuvimos
conocéis	conocisteis	estáis	estuvisteis
conocen	conocieron	están	estuvieron

HACER = to do, make	
present	*preterite*
hago	hice
haces	hiciste
hace	hizo
hacemos	hicimos
hacéis	hicisteis
hacen	hicieron

IR = to go	
present	*preterite*
voy	fui
vas	fuiste
va	fue
vamos	fuimos
vais	fuisteis
van	fueron

PREFERIR = to prefer	
present	*preterite*
prefiero	preferí
prefieres	preferiste
prefiere	prefirió
preferimos	preferimos
preferís	preferisteis
prefieren	prefirieron

QUERER = to want, love	
present	*preterite*
quiero	quise
quieres	quisiste
quiere	quiso
queremos	quisimos
queréis	quisisteis
quieren	quisieron

LEER = to read	
present	*preterite*
leo	leí
lees	leíste
lee	leyó
leemos	leímos
leéis	leísteis
leen	leyeron

PONER = to put	
present	*preterite*
pongo	puse
pones	pusiste
pone	puso
ponemos	pusimos
ponéis	pusisteis
ponen	pusieron

VOLVER = to return	
present	*preterite*
vuelvo	volví
vuelves	volviste
vuelve	volvió
volvemos	volvimos
volvéis	volvisteis
vuelven	volvieron

SENTIR = to feel	
present	*preterite*
siento	sentí
sientes	sentiste
siente	sintió
sentimos	sentimos
sentís	sentisteis
sienten	sintieron

SALIR = to go out	
present	*preterite*
salgo	salí
sales	saliste
sale	salió
salimos	salimos
salís	salisteis
salen	salieron

SER = to be	
present	*preterite*
soy	fui
eres	fuiste
es	fue
somos	fuimos
sois	fuisteis
son	fueron

Other examples of radical changing verbs which follow the above patterns, are:

cerrar = to close   pedir = to ask for
doler = to hurt   seguir = to follow / continue
empezar = to begin   torcer = to turn / follow

TENER = to have	
present	*preterite*
tengo	tuve
tienes	tuviste
tiene	tuvo
tenemos	tuvimos
tenéis	tuvisteis
tienen	tuvieron

4 Ser and Estar 'to be'

SER is used for describing permanent, unchanged things:

¿De qué nacionalidad eres?	= What nationality are you?
Soy español/a.	= I'm Spanish.

ESTAR:

- describes positions and temporary conditions:

Estoy de vacaciones.	= I am on holiday.
Mi pueblo está en el norte.	= My town is in the north.

- is used before an adjective to describe a temporary condition:

Estoy contento.	= I am happy.
Estás triste.	= You are sad.
Está ocupado.	= He /She / It / You are busy.
Estamos cansados.	= We are tired.
Estáis enfermos.	= You (plural) are ill.
Están equivocados.	= They / You (polite plural) are wrong.

- is used with a past participle to describe a state:

¿Está casado?	= Are you married?

3 Formation: Radical Changing Verbs

Other verbs follow a pattern in which the middle letters change:

JUGAR = to play	
present	*preterite*
juego	jugué
juegas	jugaste
juega	jugó
jugamos	jugamos
jugáis	jugasteis
juegan	jugaron

PODER = to be able to	
present	*preterite*
puedo	pude
puedes	pudiste
puede	pudo
podemos	pudimos
podéis	pudisteis
pueden	pudieron

5 Phrases Using Tener

There are several expressions which use **tener**. These are some of the most common:

tener … años	= to be … years old
tener calor	= to be hot
tener frío	= to be cold
tener ganas de	= to feel like
tener hambre	= to be hungry
tener miedo	= to be frightened
tener prisa	= to be in a hurry
tener razón	= to be right
tener sed	= to be thirsty
tener sueño	= to be sleepy
tener suerte	= to be lucky

In these expressions, if you want to include 'very', you must use **mucho/a**, not **muy**:

Tengo mucho/a sed.   = I am very thirsty.

6 Formation: Reflexive Verbs

Reflexive verbs have object pronouns before the different parts of the verb.

BAÑARSE = to bathe, have a bath	
present	*preterite*
me baño	me bañé
te bañas	te bañaste
se baña	se bañó
nos bañamos	nos bañamos
os bañáis	os bañasteis
se bañan	se bañaron

More verbs that follow this pattern:

acostarse	= to go to bed
dormirse	= to go to sleep
ducharse	= to have a shower
lavarse	= to (have a) wash
levantarse	= to get up
llamarse	= to be called
pasearse	= to go for a walk
tumbarse	= to lie down

Ponerse is an irregular reflexive verb:

PONERSE = to put on clothes	
present	*preterite*
me pongo	me puse
te pones	te pusiste
se pone	se puso
nos ponemos	nos pusimos
os ponéis	os pusisteis
se ponen	se pusieron

Here is a radical-changing reflexive verb:

HERIRSE = to hurt oneself	
present	*preterite*
me hiero	me herí
te hieres	te heriste
se hiere	se hirió
nos herimos	nos herimos
os herís	os heristeis
se hieren	se hieron

CONOCERSE = to know each other
¿Os conocéis? = Do you know each other?
Nos conocemos. = We know each other.

7 Present Continuous Tense

To form the present continuous tense, you take the present tense of **estar** and the present participle of the verb. To form the present participle:

- **-ar** verbs: Remove the **-ar** and add **-ando**.
- **-er** and **-ir** verbs: Remove the **-er** or the **-ir** and add **-iendo**.

Here are some verbs in the present continuous tense:

ESTUDIAR = to study	
estoy estudiando	I am studying
estás estudiando	you are studying
está estudiando	he / she / it / you (polite) are studying
estamos estudiando	we are studying
estáis estudiando	you are studying (plural)
están estudiando	they / you (polite plural) are studying

ESCRIBIR = to write	
estoy escribiendo	I am writing
estás escribiendo	you are writing
está escribiendo	he / she / it / you (polite) are writing
estamos escribiendo	we are writing
estáis escribiendo	you are writing (plural)
están escribiendo	they / you (polite plural) are writing

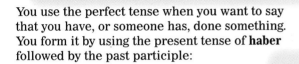

8 Perfect Tense

You use the perfect tense when you want to say that you have, or someone has, done something. You form it by using the present tense of **haber** followed by the past participle:

HABER = to have	
present	
he	I have
has	you have
ha	he / she / it / you (polite) have
hemos	we have
habéis	you have (plural)
han	they / you (polite plural) have

To form the past participle:

- **-ar** verbs: Remove the **-ar** from the infinitive and add **-ado**.
  dejar = to leave (deposit)   dejado
- **-er** and **-ir** verbs: Remove the **-er** and the **-ir** and add **-ido**.
  perder = to lose   perdido
  vivir = to live   vivido

He dejado mi maleta en la consigna.	= I have left my suitcase in left luggage.

Watch out for these irregular past participles!

infinitive	past participle
abrir = to open	abierto
decir = to speak	dicho
escribir = to write	escrito
hacer = to do, make	hecho
poner = to put	puesto
romper = to break	roto
ver = to see	visto
volver = to want	vuelto

9 Preterite Tense

The preterite tense is used to describe completed actions in the past:

See Regular, Irregular, Radical Changing Verbs and Reflexive (1, 2, 3 and 6 above) for examples.

Even if the action went on for a long time, if it is completed, the preterite must be used.

Fui a la escuela durante seis años.	= I went to primary school for six years.

10 Imperfect Tense

The imperfect tense is used to describe something which was happening, or used to happen, or for descriptions in the past:

DESAYUNAR = to have breakfast

desayun**aba**	= I was having / used to have breakfast
desayun**abas**	= you were having / used to have breakfast
desayun**aba**	= he / she / it / you (polite) was / were having / used to have breakfast
desayun**ábamos**	= we were having / used to have breakfast
desayun**abais**	= you (plural) were having / used to have breakfast
desayun**aban**	= they / you (polite plural) were having / used to have breakfast

COMER = to eat, have lunch

comía	= I was eating / used to eat
comías	= you were eating / used to eat
comía	= he / she / it / you (polite) was / were eating / used to eat
comíamos	= we were eating / used to eat
comíais	= you were eating / used to eat
comían	= they / you (polite plural) were eating / used to eat

The **-ir** verbs have the same endings as the **-er** verbs:

viv**ía**	= I was living / used to live

11 Irregular Imperfects

SER = to be	IR = to go	VER = to see
era	iba	veía
eras	ibas	veíamos
era	iba	veía
éramos	íbamos	veíamos
erais	ibais	veíais
eran	iban	veían

It is very important to be aware of the difference between the preterite and the imperfect tense:
- You must use the imperfect to describe something which was going on.
- You must use the preterite to describe something which came to interrupt it.

Learn these examples to use as models:

Cuando cruzaba la calle le atropelló el coche.	= She was crossing the street when she got run over by the car.
Mientras estábamos de compras nos encontramos con mi tía.	= While we were shopping we met my aunt.

12 Imperfect Continuous

To translate 'was … -ing', you use the imperfect continuous. It is formed by using the imperfect of **estar** with the present participle:

Estaba lloviendo.	= It was raining.

13 Phrases Using Gustar

There is no word in Spanish for 'to like'. To say that you like something or somebody, you have to say that it is pleasing to you:

Me gusta el deporte.	= I like sport.
Te gusta ir al polideportivo.	= You like going to the sports centre.
Le gusta desayunar bien.	= He / She / It / You (polite) like to have a good breakfast.
Nos gusta el español. ¿Os gusta bailar?	= We like Spanish. = Do you (plural) like dancing?
Les gustan las fiestas.	= They, you (polite plural) like the festivals.

To say that you like or someone else likes more than one thing, add an '**n**' to the end of **gusta**:

Me gustan las películas de acción.	= I like action films.
Le gustan los programas de actualidad.	= He / She / You (polite) like documentaries.

14 Personal 'a'

If a verb is followed by a person as the direct object, you insert an '**a**':

Juana lleva a Miguel en su coche.	= Juana takes Miguel in her car.
No conozco a Luisa.	= I don't know Luisa.

Watch out for these exceptions!

After **tener**: Tengo tres hermanos. = I have three brothers and sisters.

When the person is not specified: Se buscan camareros. = Wanted: Waiters

When a group of people in general is refered to: Me gustan los españoles. = I like the Spaniards.

15 Pluperfect Tense

The pluperfect tense in English is translated by the imperfect in Spanish:

Estudiaba inglés desde los doce años.	= She had studied English since she was 12.

The pluperfect tense in Spanish translates as 'has done something'. It is similar to the the perfect tense, except that the imperfect of **haber** is used instead of the present tense:

No le había visto.	= I had not seen him.

16 Future: Using 'ir a'

You can talk about what you or somebody else is going to do by using the present tense of **ir** followed by **a** and an infinitive:

Van a venir mañana.	= They are going to come tomorrow.
¿Vas a ir al cine?	= Are you going to the cinema?

17 Future Tense

If the verb is regular, you form the future by using the infinitive and the correct endings:
-é, -ás, -á, -emos, -éis, -án. Some verbs do not use their infinitives:

infinitive	future
decir = to say	diré
haber = to be	habré
hacer = to do	haré
poder = to be able	podré
querer = to want	querré
salir = to go out	saldré
tener = to have	tendré
venir = to come	vendré

El sábado visitaré a mis abuelos.	= On Saturday I will visit my grandparents.
¿Qué harás en el futuro?	= What will you do in the future?

18 Conditional Tense

The conditional is formed like the future tense, but with these endings:
-ía, -ías, -ía, -íamos, -íais, -ían.

Me gustaría ir a Escocia.	= I would like to go to Scotland.
Podrías venir en agosto.	= You could come in August.

19 Subjunctive

Use this guide to help you learn what parts of the subjunctive are relevant to your level:
* Foundation: you need to learn set phrases in the present subjunctive. E.g. ¡Qué aproveche!
* Higher: you will need to recognise all forms of the subjunctive in the Listening and Reading papers.
* You will be able to get a good grade without actually using it. Use other tenses to avoid it.
* Going for an 'A'?: learn a few phrases for each topic, especially to express opinions / reasons.

The present subjunctive
To form the present subjunctive, take the first person singular of the present tense, remove the final **o** and add the correct endings:

* **-ar verbs**: -e, -es, -e, -emos, -éis, -en.

* **-er and -ir verbs**: -a, -as, -a, -amos, - áis, -an.

Watch out!
Some verbs don't follow the rule with regard to the stem:

infinitive	present subjunctive	
dar	dé	I might give.
estar	esté	I might be.
haber	haya	I might have.
ir	vaya	I might go.
saber	sepa	I might know.
ser	sea	I might be.

When is the subjunctive used?
Here are some examples:

* Imperative: all polite forms and negative familiar forms. See also note 25.

* To express a wish:

¡Ojalá gane la lotería!	= If only I could win the lottery!
¡Qué aproveche!	= Enjoy your meal!

* After **quizás** or **tal vez** to express doubt:

Tal vez vaya al cine.	= Perhaps I'll go to the cinema.

* To express 'ought', 'might' and 'would like':

Quisiera un kilo de peras.	= I'd like a kilo of pears.

* In impersonal expressions:

No es posible que sea la verdad.	= It can't be true.

* In negative statement of 'saying', 'believing', etc.:

No creo que haya pasado nada.	= I don't think anything has happened.

* After **para que**:

Pon la radio para que pueda oír las noticias.	= Turn on the radio so that I can hear the news.

* After a verb of wanting or preferring that someone should do something, or that something should happen:

Quiero que salga el sol.	= I want the sun to shine.

* After a verb expressing emotion:

Siento que te hayan robado.	= I'm sorry you have been robbed.
Me alegro que vengas a verme.	= I'm glad you are coming to see me.

- After a verb 'asking', 'telling', 'recommending' someone to do something:

  | Le ruego me mande información. | = Please send me information. |

- After **cuando** and **en cuanto** when followed by a future idea:

  | Iré a la universidad cuando termine el colegio. | = I'll go to university when I finish school. |

- After **sin que**:

  | Cruzó la calle sin que le viera el camionero. | = She crossed the street without being seen by the lorry driver. |

- After **hasta que**:

  | Debemos quedarnos aquí hasta que deje de llover. | = We should stay here until it stops raining. |

- In an 'if' clause:

  | Me habla como si fuese una niña. | = She talks to me as if I were a child. |

- After **antes de**:

  | Quisiera pasar un año viajando antes de ir a la universidad. | = I want to spend a year travelling before I go to university. |

20 Verbs Followed by an Infinitive

When two verbs are together, with the second one in the infinitive, sometimes it is necessary to put **a**, sometimes **de**, before the infinitive. There are some common structures using verbs which take no preposition:

conseguir = to manage, get	poder = to be able to
deber = to have to	preferir = to prefer
decidir = to decide	querer = to want, wish
pensar = to think	

Quiero comer.	= I want to eat.
He conseguido un trabajo.	= I've got a job.
Prefieren ver la tele.	= They prefer to watch TV.

- Verbs which take **a**:

ayudar a = to help	ir a = to go to
empezar a = to come to	venir a = to come to
enseñar a = to show, teach	volver a = to begin again
invitar a = to invite	

  | Vengo a verte. | = I've come to see you. |
  | Ayudamos a fregar los platos. | = We help to wash up. |

- Verbs which take **de**:

  acabar de = to have just finished
  dejar de = to stop, leave off
  tener ganas de = to feel like
  terminar de = to have just stopped
  tratar de = to try to

  | Acabo de volver. | = I have just got back. |
  | Dejaré de fumar. | = I will give up smoking. |

21 Infinitives After Prepositions

In English, prepositions are often followed by the present participle of a verb. In Spanish, the infinitive is used:

al pasar por la caja	= on paying at the cash desk
antes de desayunar	= before breakfast
después de casarse	= after getting married
sin esperarles	= without waiting for them

22 Questions

In Spanish, questions start and finish with a question mark (the first is always upside down):

| ¿Puedo reservar un asiento? | = Can I reserve a seat? |

Question words have accents:

¿Dónde vives?	= Where do you live?
¿Cuándo es tu cumpleaños?	= When is your birthday?
¿Cómo eres?	= What are you like?
¿De qué nacionalidad eres?	= What is your nationality?
¿Cuál es tu color favorito?	= What is your favourite colour?
¿Cuánto es?	= How much is it?

Some of these words change to agree with plural nouns:
¿Cuáles son tus pasatiempos preferidos?
¿Quiénes son tus amigos?

These also change in order to agree with the masculine and feminine nouns that they refer to:
¿Cuántas hermanas tienes?
¿Cuántos años tienes?

¿Por qué? and porque
¿por qué ...? = why ...? (question)
porque ... = because ... (answer)
¿Por qué te gustan las ciencias?
Porque son interesantes.

23 Negatives and Affirmatives

nada = nothing
nadie = nobody
ni ... ni = neither ... nor ...
nunca / jamás = never
ninguno/a/os/as = no (adj.), none
tampoco = (n)either

When the adjective **ninguno** comes before a masculine singular noun, it loses its final **o** and becomes **ningún**:
ningún ruido | = no noise

When the negative word comes after the verb, **no** is placed before the verb:
No viene nadie. | = Nobody is coming.

If the negative word comes after the verb, **no** is not required:
Nunca como carne. | = I never eat meat.

To affirm a statement use: **sí**, **cierto**, **ciertamente**, **también**.
Sí, es cierto. | = Yes, it's true.
Juan viene también. | = Juan is coming too.

24 Por and Para

Por and **para** both mean 'for'. Use **por** to mean:

- 'on behalf of':
  Hablé por él. | = I spoke on his behalf.

- 'in exchange for':
  Pagué seis mil pesetas por los vaqueros. | = I paid 6.000 pts for the jeans.
  Gracias por la postal. | = Thanks for the postcard.

- to denote time:
  Mañana por la mañana. | = Tomorrow morning.
  Por un momento. | = For a moment.

- 'through','which', 'along':
  Paseamos por el parque. | = We strolled through the park.
  ¿Hay una farmacia por aquí? | = Is there a chemist around here?

- to denote manner or means:
  Hablar por teléfono. | = To speak on the telephone.
  Conseguí el puesto por enchufe. | = I got the job through 'string pulling'.

Use **para** for all other meanings of 'for'.

25 Imperative

Imperatives are used for giving instructions and commands.

- For a positive command, take the infinitive of a verb and remove the endings. Then add the endings given below.
- For a negative command, take the first person singular of the present tense and remove the **o**. When talking to friends, relations and children, use the **tú** and **vosotros/as** forms:

		POSITIVE	NEGATIVE
-ar	singular	-a	-es
	plural	-ad	-éis
-er	singular	-e	-as
	plural	-ed	-áis
-ir	singular	-e	-as
	plural	-id	-áis

singular | *plural*
¡Levántate! | ¡Levantaos! = Get up!
¡No te levantes! | ¡No os levantéis! = Don't get up!
¡Dame! | ¡Dadme! = Give me!
¡Cruza la plaza! | ¡Cruzad la plaza! = Cross the square!

When talking to adults who are not close friends or relatives, use **usted** and **ustedes**:

		POSITIVE	NEGATIVE
-ar	polite singular	-e	-e
	polite plural	-en	-en
-er and - ir	polite singular	-a	-a
	polite plural	-an	-an

singular | *plural*
¡Levántese! | ¡Levántense!
¡No se levante! | ¡No se levanten!
¡Deme! | ¡Denme!
¡Cruce la plaza! | ¡Cruzen la plaza!

26 Exclamations!

Note the accent on the **qué** and the upside down exclamation mark at the beginning of the exclamation:

¡Qué amable!	= How kind!
¡Qué bonito!	= How lovely!
¡Qué asco!	= How revolting!
¡Qué lástima!	= What a pity!
¡Qué zapatos tan / más bonitos!	= What nice shoes!
¡Cómo es posible!	= How is that possible!
¡Ni hablar!	= No way!

27 Passive

The passive describes the idea of an action being done to somebody or something. To form the passive, use either **ser** or **estar** followed by the past participle.

- Use **estar** to describe a state:
  El banco está cerrado.   = The bank is shut.

- Use **ser** to describe an action:
  La puerta es cerrada por el conserje.   = The door is shut by the porter.

Translate 'by' with **por**. Remember that the past participle acts like an adjective and has to agree.

How to avoid using the passive?

- Use the reflexive form:
  Se habla español.   = Spanish is spoken.

- Change the word order, changing it from passive to active:
  Un policía le entrevistó.   = A policeman interviewed him.

- Make the verb active and use the 'they' form, which makes it sound indefinite:
  Paran los pasajeros en la aduana.   = The passengers are stopped at Customs.

NOUNS

1 Gender

Nouns in Spanish are either masculine or feminine. To make nouns plural you generally add an 's'.

MASCULINE	FEMININE	PLURAL
niño	niña	niños / niñas
mano	pierna	manos / piernas
bolígrafo	goma	bolígrafos / gomas
padre	madre	padres / madres

All the above end in vowels. For nouns that end in a consonant add '**es**' to make the plural:

singular	plural
pez	**peces**
lápiz	**lápices**
camión	camion**es**
profesor	profesor**es**
árbol	árbol**es**

Some words gain or lose an accent in the plural. Words ending in '**z**' in the singular change the '**z**' to a '**c**' then add '**es**' for the plural, eg: **lápiz**, **lápices**.

2 Definite Articles

The word for 'the' changes according to whether the noun is masculine, feminine or plural:

MASCULINE	PLURAL	FEMININE	PLURAL
el hermano	**los** hermanos	la hermana	**las** hermanas

BEWARE! There are a few exceptions where nouns ending in **a** take **el**: el agua.

3 Indefinite Articles

The words for 'a', 'an' and 'some' also change:

MASCULINE	PLURAL	FEMININE	PLURAL
un amigo	unos amigos	una amiga	unas amigas

The pronoun **lo** is used in front of an adjective:

lo mejor	= the best
lo peor	= the worst
lo importante	= the important thing
lo de la lotería	= the business about the lottery

lo que is used to express 'that which', 'what':

No entiendo lo que dicen.	= I don't understand what they are saying.

When can I omit the article?

- After **tener** in most negative statements:

No tengo hermanos.	= I don't have any brothers or sisters.

- The article is omitted with nationalities and jobs:

Mi padre es cocinero.	= My father is a cook.

When do I keep the article in?

- With parts of the body:
  Me duele la cabeza. = I have a headache.
- With titles such as: el señor Ruiz, la señorita Dolores, la señora Borreguero.
- With school subjects:
  Mi gusta el inglés.

4 Articles with Verbal Nouns

The structure of **El** in front of a verb can be translated as '-ing' in certain circumstances:
El fumar es malo para la salud. = Smoking is bad for your health.

ADJECTIVES

1 Formation and Gender

Adjectives agree with the noun they describe so they also have masculine, feminine and plural forms. Remember you add '-s' to make the adjective plural.

MASCULINE	PLURAL	FEMININE	PLURAL
negro	negros	negra	negras
guapo	guapos	guapa	guapas
el chico guapo	los chicos guapos	la chica guapa	las chicas guapas

Most adjectives end in 'o' for masculine and 'a' for feminine.

BEWARE!
Here are a few of the many exceptions:

MASCULINE	PLURAL	FEMININE	PLURAL
inteligente	inteligentes	inteligente	inteligentes
grande	grandes	grande	grandes
azul	azules	azul	azules
gris	grises	gris	grises

Adjectives of nationality ending in a consonant in their masculine singular add '**-a**' for the feminine singular and '**as**' for the feminine plural.

singular	*plural*
el chico es español	los chicos son españoles
la chica es española	las chicas son españolas

Watch out!
There are some adjectives which lose the final '**o**' in front of a masculine singular noun:

bueno, buen	Hace buen tiempo.
malo, mal	Hace mal tiempo.
primero, primer	el primer ministro
tercero, tercer	el tercer piso
alguno, algún	algún día
ninguno, ningún	ningún deporte

2 Position

Some adjectives change their meaning according to their position, **mismo** and **pobre** being common examples:

Es el mismo vestido.	= It's the same dress.
Yo mismo voy.	= I'm going myself.
Pobre Miguel.	= Poor Miguel.
Es un país pobre.	= It's a poor country.

Grande loses its **-de** when in front of any singular noun and in this case it changes its meaning from 'big' to 'great'.

Picasso es un gran pintor.	= Picasso is a great painter.
Cuidad de México es una ciudad grande.	= Mexico City is a big city.

3 Possessive Adjectives

The words for 'my', 'your', 'his' and 'her' are the same for both masculine and feminine. You add an 's' to make them plural:

	SINGULAR		PLURAL	
	Masculine/Feminine		Masculine/Feminine	
my your (tú) your (usted)	**mi** libro **tu** cuaderno **su** bolígrafo		**mis** libros **tus** cuadernos **sus** bolígrafos	
	Masculine	Feminine	Masculine	Feminine
our your	**nuestro** ordenador **vuestro** ordenador	**nuestra** casa **vuestra** casa	**nuestros** pupitres **vuestros** pupitres	**nuestras** sillas **vuestras** sillas
	Masculine/Feminine		Masculine/Feminine	
their / your (ustedes)	**su** dormitorio		**sus** dormitorios	

4 Demonstrative Adjectives

The words for 'this', 'these', 'that', 'those' and 'that/those over there' agree with the nouns they describe:

MASCULINE
este sombrero
ese abrigo
aquel jersey

PLURAL
estos sombreros
esos abrigos
aquellos jerseys

FEMININE
esta camisa
esa bufanda
aquella corbata

PLURAL
estas camisas
esas bufandas
aquellas botas

ADVERBS

1 Adverbs as Quantifiers

To describe quantity and degree, use quantifiers. These are some example:

muy	Es muy rico. = It's very tasty.
poco	Tengo poco dinero. = I don't have much money.
mucho	Hizo mucho frío. = It was very cold.
demasiado	He bebido demasiado. = I have drunk too much.
bastante	He comido bastante. = I have eaten enough.

2 Formation and Gender

Take the feminine form of the adjective and add **-mente**. E.g. básica – básicamente.

> **Watch out for this exception!**
> Some adverbs don't end in **-mente.** E.g. bien, mal, despacio.

If two adverbs are used together, **-mente** is added only to the second one. E.g. Trabaja rápida y inteligentemente.

3 Comparatives and Superlatives

barato/a = cheap
rápido/a = fast
más barato/a = cheaper
más rápidamente = faster
el/la más barato/a = the cheapest
lo más rápidamente = the fastest

Belén es más alta que José.	= Belén is taller than José.
Los precios más baratos de la ciudad.	= The cheapest prices in town.

Menos translates as 'less' or 'not so':

Es menos caro.	= It is less expensive.

Tan … como translates as 'as … as …':

Ir en tren es más cómodo que ir en autocar.	= Going by train is more comfortable than going by coach.

BEWARE!
There are two special forms of **grande**, depending on the meaning:

grande = big
más grande = bigger
el más grande = the biggest
el mayor = the greatest, the oldest

grande = great
mayor = greater, older

Watch out for these irregular adverbs!

bien = well
mejor = better
lo mejor = the best
mucho = much
más = more
lo más = the most

mal = bad
peor = worse
el peor = the worst
poco = little
menos = less
lo menos = the least

-ísimo at the end of an adjective translates as 'very', 'most'. E.g. corto – cortísimo, bueno – buenísimo, rico – riquísimo. (Note the spelling changes.)

4 Diminutives

These are used to indicate smallness. They are formed by adding either of these endings:

-ito (-cito, -ecito, -ececito) and **-illo** (-cillo, -ecillo, -ececillo).

- **-ito** is the most common and can also indicate affection:

Juan — Juanito
señora — señorita
pueblo — pueblecito
cuchara — cucharita

BEWARE!
-illo can also be pejorative. E.g. hombre – hombrecillo, pan – panecillo, ventana – ventanilla. (Note the spelling changes.)

5 Augmentatives

These are used less than diminutives:
-ón, **-ona** is the most common and indicates an increase in size or quality.
-azo, **-uza** indicates disproportionate size.
-ote, **-ota** is usually used to make something appear monstrous or ridiculous.

guapo — guapetón
gente — gentuza

PRONOUNS

1 Demonstrative Pronouns

These follow the same pattern as demonstrative adjectives, but notice the accents:

MASCULINE
éste es mi tío
ése es mi abuelo
aquél es mi padre

PLURAL
éstos son mis tíos
ésos son mis abuelos
aquéllos son mis padres

FEMININE
ésta es mi prima
ésa es mi hermana
aquélla es mi sobrina

PLURAL
éstas son mis primas
ésas son mis hermanas
aquéllas son mis sobrinas

2 Relative Pronouns

'Who' or 'what' translates as **que**. 'Whom' translates as **que** or **a quien(es)**:
El tren que va a Sevilla. = The train which goes to Seville.

'Whose' is translated as **cuyo/a/s**:
El amigo cuya moto voy a comprar. = The friend whose motorbike I am going to buy.

'Which' after a preposition is expressed in either of the following ways:

Masculine	Masculine	Feminine	Feminine
singular	plural	singular	plural
el que **el cual**	**los que** **los cuales**	**la que** **la cual**	**las que** **las cuales**

It agrees with the noun to which it refers:

No importa cuales.	= It doesn't matter which.

Lo que translates as 'what' in the middle of a sentence:

Sé lo que están diciendo.	= I know what they are saying.

3 Subject Pronouns

SINGULAR		PLURAL		
		Masculine	Feminine	
yo	I	nosotros (m)	nosotras (f)	we
tú (familiar)	you	vosotros (m)	vosotras (f)	you
él	he / it	ellos (m)	ellas (f)	they
ella	she / it			
usted	you (polite)	ustedes	ustedes	you (polite)

4 Direct Object Pronouns

SINGULAR		PLURAL	
me	me	nos	us
te	you	os	you (plural)
le / lo	you (polite) / him / it	les / los	them / you (polite)
la	you (polite) / her / it	las	them / you (polite)

5 Indirect Object Pronouns

SINGULAR		PLURAL	
me	to me	nos	to us
te	to you	os	you (plural)
le	to you (polite) / him / her / it / you	les	them / you (polite)

The object pronouns are placed immediately before the verb:

Lo compra. = He buys it.
Nos hablan. = They speak to us.
No te comprendo. = I don't understand you.

The object pronoun is joined on to the end of the verb in certain cases:
- infinitives: Viene a verlo. = He is coming to see it.
- present participles: Estoy comiéndolo. = I am eating it.
- commands: Escuchadme. = Listen to me.

When two object pronouns are together – one direct, the other indirect – the indirect always goes before the direct:

Va a dármelo. = He is going to give it to me.

Explíquemelo. = Explain it to me

When **le** or **les** comes before **lo**, **la**, **los** and **las**, you change the **le** or **les** to **se**:

Se lo doy. = I give it to him.

When two verbs are together, with the second one in the infinitive, object pronouns can either be put on the end of the infinitive or placed in front of the verb:

Se la voy a prestar.
OR Voy a prestársela. = I am going to introduce her to him.

6 Possessive Pronouns

	SINGULAR	
	Masculine	Feminine
mine	el mío	la mía
yours	el tuyo	la tuya
his / hers / yours (polite)	el suyo	la suya
ours	el nuestro	la nuestra
yours (plural)	el vuestro	la vuestra
theirs / yours (polite plural)	el suyo	la suya

	PLURAL	
	Masculine	Feminine
mine	los míos	las mías
yours	los tuyos	las tuyas
his / hers / yours (polite)	los suyos	las suyas
ours	los nuestros	las nuestras
yours (plural)	los vuestros	las vuestras
theirs / yours (polite plural)	los suyos	las suyas

El / La/s suyo/a/s have six possible meanings. To avoid confusion, they can be replaced by **de él, de ella, de Vd., de ellos, de ellas, de Vds.**:

No me gusta su chaqueta. = I don't like his jacket.
Prefiero la de ella. I prefer hers.

When the possessive pronoun comes immediately after a part of **ser**, you leave out the definite article:

Esa bolsa es suya. = That bag is his.
OR Esa bolsa es de él.

7 Strong Pronouns

mí	me	nosotros	us
ti	you	vosotros	you (plural)
él	him / it	ellos	them (masculine)
ella	her / it	ellas	them (feminine)
Vd	you (polite)	Vds.	you (polite plural)
sí *	oneself		

para mí = for me
con ellos = with them

* Sí is not commonly used but it is useful to recognise it. It means: oneself, himself, herself, yourself (formal); themselves, yourselves (formal) when it refers back to the subject of the sentence.

Estaba fuera de sí.	= She was beside herself (with worry).

PREPOSITIONS

a la derecha de = to the right of
a la izquierda de = to the left of

dentro de = inside	detrás de = behind
al lado de = next to	enfrente de = opposite
debajo de = under	fuera de = outside
delante de = in front of	sobre = on top of

El banco está al lado del supermercado.	= The bank is next to the supermarket.

Remember that **a** + **el becomes al**, and that **de** + **el** becomes del.

- **desde** = since

This is used with the present tense in Spanish where in English you would use the perfect tense:

Estoy aquí desde las 9h 00.	= I have been here since 9.00.

- **desde hace** = for

¿Desde hace cuánto tiempo estudias español?	= How long have you been studying Spanish?

Estudio español desde hace tres años.	= I have been studying Spanish for three years.

- **acabar de** = to have just

This is followed by a verb in the infinitive:

Acabamos de mudarnos de casa.	= We have just moved house.

NUMBERS

- **Uno** becomes **un** before a noun:
  Un hermano.
- **Cien** becomes **ciento** when it is followed or preceded by another number:
  Cien gramos de jamón serrano. **Ciento** cincuenta gramos de chorizo.
- To name a year in Spanish, you do not break up the number of the year into two as in English:
  mil cuatrocientos noventa y dos = 1492
- **Primero** becomes **primer** before a masculine noun:
  El primer piso.
  Primera remains the same:
  la primera vez.
- **Dates**
  el primero / dos / tres de mayo = (May 1st / 2nd / 3rd)

Ordinal Numbers

1º/ª	primero/a	6º/ª	sexto/a
2º/ª	segundo/a	7º/ª	séptimo/a
3º/ª	tercero/a	8º/ª	octavo/a
4º/ª	cuarto/a	9º/ª	noveno/a
5º/ª	quinto/a	10ª/º	décimo/a

1^0 = el primero (m) / 1^a = la primera (f) = first

el último (m) / la última (f) = last

Ordinal numbers after 10th are rarely used in Spanish. Instead you use the cardinal numbers after the noun. E.g. el siglo veintiuno = the 21st century.

12

WRITING

1 Spelling Changes

Certain rules in Spanish cause changes in the spelling of words, particularly with verbs:

z changes to **c** when followed by **e** or **i**.
Crucé la calle.   = I crossed the street.

g changes to **gu** when followed by **e** or **i**.
Pagué la cuenta.   = I paid the bill.

c (hard) changes to **qu** when followed by **e** or **i**.
No te acerques al fuego.   = Don't go near the fire.

g (soft) changes to **j** when not followed by **e** or **i**.
Coja el tran.   = Get / catch the train.

gu changes to **g** when not followed by **e** or **i**.
Siga por la calle.   = Carry on down the street.

l changes to **y** when it is unstressed and comes between two vowels
Cayó al suelo.   = It fell on the floor.

2 Accents

The accent on an **ñ/Ñ** indicates that you must pronounce the **n** as '**ny**'. The only other accent in Spanish is like the acute accent, e.g. ú. Follow these rules when deciding whether to use an accent:

- If a word ends in a vowel, **n** or **s**, the stress falls on the last but one syllable. E.g. buscamos, hablas, mesa, preguntan, pupitre, trabajaba.
- If the word ends in a consonant (apart from **n** or **s**), the stress is on the last syllable: andaluz, azul, desayunar, escuchad, Madrid, venir.
- If the pronunciation of the word means that either of the above rules is broken, an accent must be placed over the stressed vowel. E.g. bailó, buzón, comía, francés, película, vendría.
- Question words: ¿cómo?, ¿cuál?, ¿cuándo?, ¿cuántos?, ¿qué?, ¿quién?.
- When two words with different meanings are spelt the same, one of them carries an accent:
  sí = yes, si = if
  mí = me, mi = my
  él = him, el = the

Congratulations! Have you worked through the ten topics chapters, the colour Mind Maps and the grammar reference section? And how did you do in the mock exam in Chapter 11? If you have made the most of this Spanish Revision Guide you will be able to do your best in the GCSE exam. It is a good idea to have a closer look at the way that the exam grades are calculated. Look again at page 13. If you know how the examiner works, you can aim for a better grade.

So if your exam is tomorrow have a bath now and relax. Make sure you are feeling calm about the exam. As a last boost why not browse through the Mind Maps in this book and look at those you have drawn yourself. Good luck!

Index